Selling
by Phone

How to Reach and Sell Customers
in the Nineties

Linda Richardson

McGraw-Hill, Inc.

New York   San Francisco   Washington, D.C.   Auckland   Bogotá
Caracas   Lisbon   London   Madrid   Mexico City   Milan
Montreal   New Delhi   San Juan   Singapore
Sydney   Tokyo   Toronto

Library of Congress Cataloging-in-Publication Data

Richardson, Linda, date.
   Selling by phone : how to reach and sell customers in the nineties /
Linda Richardson.
        p.   cm.
   Includes index.
   ISBN 0-07-052339-8 (hc)   ISBN 0-07-052376-2 (pbk)
   1. Telephone selling.   I. Title.
HF5438.3.R527   1992
658.8′4–dc20   91-41277
                                                            CIP

First McGraw-Hill paperback edition, 1994

  4 5 6 7 8 9 0 DOC/DOC 9 8 7 6 5 4   (HC)
  11 12 13 14 15 16 DOC/DOC 0 9 8 7 6 5 4 3 2   (PBK)

ISBN 0-07-052339-8 (HC)
ISBN 0-07-052376-2 (PBK)

*The sponsoring editor for this book was Theodore C. Nardin, the editing
supervisor was Stephen M. Smith, and the production supervisor was Suzanne
W. Babeuf. It was set in Baskerville by McGraw-Hill's Professional Book
Group composition unit.*

Printed and bound by R. R. Donnelley & Sons Company.

 This book is printed on recycled, acid-free paper containing a
minimum of 50% recycled, de-inked fiber.

In memory of my father:
"si et vivo carus amicis;
causa fuit pater his…"

Horace, Satires *1.6, lines 70–71*

Contents

Preface

Selling by phone is worlds apart from telemarketing. A lack of consultative selling skills that often borders on harassment has given telemarketing such a stigma that even many top *salespeople* cringe when they hear the word. Consider Al, a warm, ethical, intelligent, retired salesman. We were discussing selling, and it was clear he loved it. I mentioned that my next book would be on telephone selling and all his exuberant conversation subsided. His expression changed as he settled into dead silence. Then he said, "No, I don't like selling over the telephone." "Why?" I asked, and he discussed calls he got at home pushing products — including calls generated by computers. I explained that was *not* what my book was about. This book was for salespeople and other business people who use the phone as part of the sales process. He brightened up and admonished me to make that clear in my title. Hence the title communicates to salespeople and non-salespeople alike that I'm talking about using the telephone to *bring in* and *build* relationships, not scare them off or tear them down.

Today telephone selling is an integral part of the selling process. Telephone selling can be as consultative and relationship-oriented as face-to-face selling, which it may or may not include. Whether you are on the phone pretty much all day with clients or you use the phone to supplement face-to-face sales calls, you need this "extension" of yourself to sell. No longer can any sales professional rely strictly on face-to-face selling. Even salespeople who once used the telephone solely to make face-to-face appointments or to follow up on face-to-face contacts now use the telephone actively in the sales process. The combination of a global marketplace, tough competitors, sophisticated and demanding clients, and unprecedented technology has created a sales environment that demands the kind of on-the-spot responsiveness possible with the phone. Whether you use the telephone to make the initial contact, qualify, answer last-minute questions, calm client fears, close the deal, or all the above, today the phone is indispensable to you if you are to expand client relationships profitably and build new ones.

The phone is key in all phases of the sale—from introducing an idea to testing the waters to closing. With the phone you can reach clients, present ideas, get feedback, move things along, stay in touch, finalize details, negotiate, and close. You can even comply with legal requirements to communicate the availability of your offer to *all* customers regardless of size. In today's volatile market, the phone often is the only effective way to address constant change. Of course, there will *always* be situations that demand face-to-face contact, but even these—indeed, especially these—demand phone contact to make deals happen.

Successful salespeople who sell over the phone operate within the same consultative sales framework—*opening, needs, positioning, objections, closing, follow-up*—and use the same consultative selling skills—*presence, relating, questioning, listening, positioning, checking*—as they do in effective face-to-face selling. Yet how the framework functions and how salespeople use these skills differ in response to a different medium. Although these differences often are subtle, they are critical to success.

The main difference between face-to-face and telephone selling is obvious. Over the phone, the salesperson is not physically present. There is no face-to-face contact—no eye contact, no handshake, no physical "presence." And as psychologists and sociologists have known for decades, there can be a sense of anonymity and depersonalization with the phone. It is this potential for depersonalization that creates the bulk of the important sales differences to you as a salesperson. To compensate for this, your voice, your choice of words, and your ability to build rapport, question, and listen to subvocal messages and hesitations or enthusiasm all take on added importance.

Telephone selling has a reality of its own. It can be more challenging than face-to-face selling because of the lack of personal contact. You can't *see* the client, much less the client's reaction. This invisibility gives the client more freedom. The same customer who would feel obliged to hear you out politely in person might deal with you on the telephone by being distant, being unfriendly, hanging up, or avoiding your call altogether. The clients or prospects being called can become defensive because they usually have no way to prepare for the call and so feel that they lack control. The controversy of caller ID (a phone feature in which the people being called have the option of seeing the numbers of the persons or organizations calling them) versus phone blocking (in which some phone numbers could be masked) centers on this very issue of preparation and control of calls. To complicate the matter further, there is often less time, less flexibility, and less *commitment* over the phone. For example, the client who flies to Chicago from Seattle to meet with you or agrees to have you come there, under most circumstances, has made a far greater commitment to you than the client who takes your call. *Telephone* selling skills are needed to compensate for these differences.

In spite of all these challenges, knowing *how* to sell over the phone can have big payoffs. This is as true for salespeople *without* the sales title *salesperson* such as CEOs, executives, and politicians as it is for people who carry the title of *salesperson* directly or indirectly such as investment bankers, consultants, and sales representatives. That psychotherapy, social services, and even love affairs can be conducted over the phone shows that intimate relationships can be developed and carried on by phone. In fact, many selling situations can be *better served* by phone than face to face if the salesperson knows how to compensate for the differences inherent in telephone selling. To maximize the potential of the phone as a tool for selling, you need to refine your face-to-face selling skills to this "next" level.

The purpose of this book is to help you *build on*, *expand*, and *polish* your present selling skill — both natural and trained — so that you can maximize the phone as a tool for building relationships with clients and increasing your production. If you presently use the phone as a part of your sales process, you have already developed many of the skills you need. If you are not maximizing the potential of the phone to sell, hopefully the ideas in this book will save you time and help you improve your skills to make you more effective. This book will increase your awareness of what you are or are not doing when you are on the phone as a way to help you refine your *existing* skills. This book will also help you understand the difference between consultative and product selling, provide an understanding of the framework of a phone sales call, sharpen the six critical skills you need to sell over the phone, and help you make a more informed decision as to when and when not to use the phone.

Linda Richardson

Overview

The Telephone as a Power Tool for Selling

The phone allows you to be *more responsive* and *more active* with your clients and prospects because it enables you to keep in touch more frequently. You can use the phone minute to minute, hour to hour, day by day, or month to month to transact business, respond to changes in the market, and strengthen and expand your relationships.

Even businesses that in the past relied on face-to-face selling as their primary mode of selling—that used the phone only to arrange face-to-face appointments—today use the phone to sell from opening to close. There is almost *no limit* to the business that can be done by phone today. You can use the phone to:

- Prospect
- Qualify a prospect
- Qualify a client

- Introduce an idea
- Sell a product (*close* the sale over the telephone)
- Reach more clients or prospects in a shorter period, reducing sales costs
- Reach the smaller client you can't afford to call on
- Piggy-back a sales call on to a call to communicate other information such as a change
- Negotiate terms
- Finalize a detail of a transaction
- Test an idea with a client and/or get feedback
- Cross-sell and/or expand the relationship
- Bring new information to the client or provide up-to-the-minute market information
- Keep all levels in the account informed
- Arrange for referrals by getting approval from and preparing your present clients for calls from prospects
- Follow up
- *Prepare* for a meeting — develop an agenda, what will be covered, who will be there, etc.
- Answer client questions
- Arrange a face-to-face appointment
- Arrange a *telephone* appointment
- Solve problems
- Calm client fears ("You may have seen the article in the newspaper. . . . We are . . . ")
- Save a relationship
- Respond to client complaints
- Arrange social/business activities (such as inviting a client to a game or concert — no harm in mentioning that deal, tactfully)
- Collect
- Make relationship calls ("How am I doing?"/ "Happy Thanksgiving."/"Hello.")

You don't have to have a business reason to call. You can simply build warm, friendly relationships over time by showing clients you are thinking about them.

Consultative Telephone Selling for the Nineties

Before we look at some very practical how-to's for successful telephone selling, let's consider the special challenges all salespeople face in the nineties. Salespeople are selling in a world of expanding competition, a world that is increasingly cluttered with look-alike products. In this environment, product selling—long *the* way to sell—is no longer viable. Salespeople who sell by telling a *product* story will have a hard time differentiating their products or ideas from their competitors, since most product stories today, competitor-to-competitor, sound alike. Products look alike not only to customers but also to salespeople. The assistant treasurer of a major corporation, a sophisticated buyer, recently said in *Institutional Investor* that, in interviewing six competitors for a banking service, he saw "the same product with six different names."

Even salespeople with leading edge products will need superior skills and superior knowledge to gain an edge because competitors can copy and eclipse products in a few months—or even a single hour. In addition, salespeople today are facing a tough business climate in which, although there is business out there, there is generally *less* of it. For all these reasons, salespeople must develop superior skills in going after and winning as much of the profitable business as possible.

Sales success in this environment requires a small but radical shift in selling—an about-face, or, more accurately, an "about-ear" change, from product selling to consultative selling. Although most salespeople say they are consultative—truly oriented to client needs—many still engage in product selling they could do blindfolded! Product selling—tell your product story, present your features and benefits—continues to masquerade as consultative selling as almost everyone pays lip service to consultative selling. The truth is that the product-sell approach is hard to shake. It is the role model most salespeople (and sales *trainers*) were trained in, and training – good or bad – dies hard. Many salespeople who see themselves as consultative are surprised when they observe themselves on our training videos *hammering away at their products* and talking much more than they are listening.

Consider one telephone salesperson, industrious and proactive, who reached the president of a company at 8:30 a.m. About 10 seconds into the conversation, the dialogue (like a thousand other dialogues) went like this:

> PROSPECT: "I'm not interested."
>
> SALESPERSON: "Well, don't you want to save money?"

Within a few moments, the prospect was off the line. Why? Why not! The client disengaged because he "felt" a product dump (pitch) coming and escaped! The salesperson making this call probably intended to be consultative by focusing on the client's needs. But he, like countless other salespeople, didn't have the skill level to be consultative.

What was the problem? What could the salesperson possibly have said to change the course of the call, to gain the prospect's interest, qualify him, find out what his situation was, and possibly get to the next step? The salesperson had a few seconds with this prospect, and he used his time the best way he knew how. He tried using – or should I say "masquerading" – a client benefit question, but he lost an opportunity. His "question" – "Well, don't you want to save money?" – was a turn-off. Think about it. Think too about the prospect's objection. Listen to it: "I'm not interested." What does this really mean? It is as much a knee-jerk reaction as a real description of the client's situation. The client might just as well have said, "We just bought X . . . " or "I have a brother-in-law in the business. . . . " These objections may sound specific, but they are really *very* general. These objections are *generic* – most client objections are. To compound this problem, most salespeople's instinct is to respond to a generic objection with a generic response. The 8:30 a.m. salesperson's response was generic. He or she might as well have said, "But we have a new product line" or the old tried-but-no-longer-true, "*If*

I could show you . . . would you. . . . " The salesperson used a *leading* question hoping to get a chance to tell his product story. But what is clear is that there was no direct relationship between what the client said and how the salesperson responded: Each was speaking the vague language of the no-sale sales dialogue.

To understand how the salesperson handled this objection, consider for a moment the three basic types of salespeople we have identified based on our 15 years of training thousands and thousands of salespeople from associate to senior levels:

- Product salespeople
- Product-application salespeople
- Consultative salespeople

Product salespeople talk about their products. They talk and talk and talk about their products. Almost all new salespeople go through this phase; it is the new salesperson's equivalent to childhood's "terrible twos." Either salespeople evolve through this stage or they get out of selling. If they progress through the phase, they eventually figure out that they need to let the client talk. But when they reach this realization, they then evolve into — and get stuck in — the second phase, product-application selling. (This seems to be the case with our 8:30 salesman, since he at least asked a question.)

Product-application salespeople are more complex to analyze than product salespeople because there are so many gradations in this group. This group of salespeople identifies and responds to "surface" customer needs but relatively quickly focuses on the product. Product application salespeople range from fair to good to very good to very, very good. Many of these salespeople have plaques of achievement on their walls, and many earn substantial incomes. But sooner or later during the sales contact (usually sooner), they focus on their product (what they are selling), not on the client's solution.

In an industrywide study, one client organization was rated by its customers as number one and its competitor a close number two *except* in the category of "consulting," where the competitor was number one. The management of the group realized that this one area of weakness could eventually lead to the organization's fall from grace from first to second place. Diagnosis revealed that the salespeople in this group of cash management specialists were knowledgeable in their area of expertise but lacked an understanding of overall related client needs. They looked at their client as the client pertained to their products, instead of looking at their products as they pertained to their client. Their product-focus approach failed to address the customer's full needs. The new electronic cash management products offered benefits companywide, not just in the treasury area. Product knowledge was not the solution to this problem; client knowledge was! We found that these salespeople had great products and excellent product knowledge, but they knew very little about their client's business or strategy and the "list" of questions they asked, while consistent, was narrowly focused.

Consultative salespeople, however, focus on the *client* (what the client wants to achieve), and they *keep* their focus there. This is deceptively simple! There is a subtle but substantive difference between what product-application salespeople do and what consultative salespeople do. A product-application salesperson cannot successfully compete with consultative salespeople when other factors are equal. Consultative salespeople are different from product-oriented salespeople in many ways. They are also rare—our experience shows them to be about 1 in 30. Whenever we meet or hear of one of these *top* performers, we make an effort to interview them to find out what it is they do and what makes them so successful. Most of them tell us the same things, over and over. They know their clients—first and foremost. Integrity is also high on their list. They tell us their clients can count on them. These salespeople say they deliver what they promise—often making the point that they deliver *more* than they promise. They can get things done internally where their colleagues get bogged down with uncooperative colleagues or limited resources. The top performers have strong informal, internal networks which allow them to bring the resources of their organizations literally to their clients' doorsteps.

Attitude is another winning factor. These successful salespeople *believe in their products* and are confident they can add value. When we ask them about their skills and how they sell, they talk about things like *listening* and taking notes. When we observe them, we find they ask *more* questions, deeper questions. They don't give up, and they follow up. And excellent product knowledge for them is a given!

Let me give you an example of a consultative salesperson. My husband is a physician who buys medical equipment from a variety of companies, including General Electric. He and I were invited to dinner with his G.E. sales representative and the rep's sales manager. The sales manager was very impressive. I suppose because my business is sales training, the conversation eventually turned to selling. His ideas were very helpful. Several weeks later when I ran into the salesman, I mentioned how much I enjoyed meeting his sales manager. He said, "Oh, he's a *legend* at G.E." He then relayed this story to me: The previous month the sales manager was in the Far East when one of their competitors presented a film that was superior to G.E.'s. The group from G.E. felt a bit crestfallen, but they managed to make the appropriate complimentary remarks. When it was the sales manager's turn to look at the film, he not only complimented the quality, he identified a disease pictured in one of the slides—a rare bone disease peculiar to Asia. This diagnosis created a hush around the table and helped rebalance the scales. While this example is extreme, it reaffirms what these top performers tell us over and over—they know their clients' business.

Actually in many ways the line between an effective product-application salesperson and a consultative salesperson is a fine one, but that line means the difference between winning the business or watching while your competitor wins the business. Today few contenders win by a mile; wins are often by a nose, by a photo finish, and consultative selling helps give that edge.

Consider the play *Death of a Salesman* by Arthur Miller. Miller's story is about the human experience of a salesperson who had once been successful in sales but no longer was. Several years ago Miller accepted an invitation to direct this play in China. He knew the challenges ahead—the political barriers and the language barriers. Critics were afraid the theme, the failure of a U.S. salesman, would not be understood outside the United States. Yet it was. The playwright's job was to transmit that feeling of failure, and he did just that. One of my favorite lines describes Willy Loman, the main character of the play, as "riding on a smile and a shoeshine." This line tells why Willy failed. The world changed but he didn't. In 1949, when this play was written, sales was turning from personality *to* product selling. In 1949 customers were no longer persuaded by smiles—they wanted product knowledge, and Willy was left behind because he did not adapt. What we can learn from the play is that being out of step with the times was a concept universally understood by people all over the world. When markets, customers, and products change, sales organizations and salespeople must change too, to survive.

Today we are at another turning point in sales, and the product, far from being the differentiator, is the equalizer. A few decades ago clients were hungry for "product." They were eager to hear product stories. They listened. Salespeople could "educate" them. From the fifties to the early eighties, the product could be counted on as a key differentiator. But in today's competitive environment, the key to differentiation is the client.

Consultative selling allows salespeople to put the emphasis on the client; consultative salespeople know *how* to do this. Today's sales equation for success—for top performance—is more demanding than ever. An English client told me that, "It takes *more* than a McClean's smile and a good menu of products to win a deal today." He was right. Success in selling today hinges on differentiation largely *outside* the product—in the salesperson, in her or his organization, in knowledge of the client, and in value-added elements such as history, quality, service, expertise, creativity, reputation, and focus on what the client wants to achieve.

Consultative selling boils down to the ability of the salesperson to relate and question, and although this sounds simple, it is not. Old molds don't break easily. In the past, selling was talking. Today, selling is listening first. This takes awareness, discipline, skill, skill, and more skill.

Let's go back to our 8:30 a.m. salesperson. He might have met with more success had he really tried to help the client or tried to understand the client's thinking. Unless the salesperson has a crystal ball, he or she would have had to ask questions. The one thing you can be sure of in sales is that you won't *sell* (not order taking) to anyone if you don't know how she or he thinks. The words you use are not the issue, but your approach is. Had the 8:30 salesman shown empathy and asked a "why" question, he may have opened some doors. For example, he might have asked, "Mr. . . . , I can appreciate your not being interested (empathy). Since we offer savings over . . . to clients like you (potential benefit) . . . *may I ask why you are not interested?*" This is *not* a trick question, since the salesperson really can't be helpful if he doesn't know the answer.

If there were a chance to sell to this prospect, it might have been discovered through the process of empathy and why questioning — certainly more than with the transparent tactic of "Don't you want to save money?" Perhaps with a question really designed to know what was going on, an opening could have been created. Perhaps the prospect might have said, "I don't handle this. Call X if there are real savings. Goodbye." Even if the client had responded to the money question with, "How much money will I save?" (which is highly unlikely), discussing price at this point would be premature. Discussing price would have bypassed what should have been a short sales dialogue: What do you need, and what do we have to match up with that need? In today's environment, clients must be brought more actively into the selling process. They need to "teach" you how to sell to them. The sales monologue must give way to a sales dialogue, and the products focus must be transformed to a client focus.

Now let's look first at the general framework of a telephone sales call to understand the structure of the consultative approach and then at the six critical consultative telephone selling skills that can help you close more sales and open up key relationships.

Framework and Critical Skills for Telephone Sales Calls

If you were to listen in on a series of "excellent" consultative telephone sales calls, you would find that certain elements would consistently appear in each call. Although the clients, products, and the style of the salesperson in each call would be different, there would be six basic elements in each call. Not surprisingly, these six elements are:

- Opening
- Client needs
- Product match-up/positioning of ideas
- Objections and resolution of objections
- Closing/action step
- Follow-up

These elements may seem easy and self-evident, but most sales-people trip up in one or more of them, throwing themselves off the sales trail and off the time.

These six elements are the structure or skeleton of a telephone call. They don't occur in a fixed sequence. For example, telephone clients often object as you open. And since telephone selling can often involve a series of closely timed calls (such as several calls in one hour for a swap) or follow-up calls in which one call may pick up where the last call left off, all elements of the framework may not be a part of every call. Also, in telephone selling some calls are "get it done" calls and others are "paving the way" relationship calls. *So there are no steps per se.* This is one of the big differences between traditional selling of the past versus selling in the 1990s. Selling is no longer linear—it just doesn't happen that way—not with today's customers. Of course, the opening comes first and the close comes at the end, but since today's clients won't normally sit cooperatively while you go through a series of "steps," you need a flexible process and excellent skills to involve the client yet still stay in control of the call. How well or poorly the call goes is largely a function of your skills—six critical ones. These skills are to the framework what your muscles are to your skeleton—they provide strength and flexibility. The six critical selling skills are:

- Presence
- Relating
- Questioning
- Listening

- Positioning

- Checking

These six critical skills are used *throughout* each element of the framework — for example, *all* six skills are used as you open; all are used as you deal with objections; all are used as you identify needs; and all are used as you close. The six elements are the skeletal structure, but the six critical skills are the muscle, the momentum. The six critical skills are what gets things moving and the deal done.

The only sequence for selling you need to master is simply this: Make sure that you understand client needs before you talk at any length or depth about your products or ideas. This is much easier said than done. For example, this idea of finding needs before telling your product story was discussed in one of our recent sales seminars. As usual, everyone agreed and felt the *review* of such an elementary principle was unnecessary — it was too obvious, too basic. Then came the practice, where, as they say, "the rubber hits the road." The role play went like this — two minutes into the telephone call about a payroll processing system:

> CLIENT: "I don't want to change."
>
> SALESPERSON: "I can understand your being satisfied with your present system. But our system is superior and I think we can offer you many advantages. Can your system address your needs for the future?"

Snapshot Analysis of Salesperson's Response. The salesperson gave it her best. First, on the positive side, she showed empathy as she began to respond to the objection: "I can understand . . . system." Second, she did ask a question — "Can your system address your needs for the future?" She also believed in her product, and her tone was nondefensive.

However, her response was ineffective. She began by contradicting the client: "But our system is superior and. . . ." She risked offending the client. She was making an unsubstantiated claim. What was she basing her claim of superiority on? She then proceeded to ask a question not to be helpful but to put doubt in the client's mind about the client's system's ability to handle future needs. This question might be fine—later! She didn't know his present system, and the client knew it! Her question was flawed in two ways: (1) it was closed-end, eliciting a yes or no answer; *more* important, (2) it was a question designed to show the client he was wrong, not to find out how he was thinking and why!

Like the 8:30 salesperson, this salesperson's response was a good example of product push! The salesperson went to the *product*, not to the client. This is the way *most* salespeople sell. But you can be different. You can be the 1 in 30 who are truly consultative.

On pp. 15 and 16 each phrase the salesperson uttered is looked at in depth and an alternative mind set is considered. It is not so much that what the salesperson said was wrong; it just wasn't good enough for today's competitive environment. The salesperson in this example was a good performer, but she fell into a common product-application trap. She was too fast on the trigger, *putting solutions before needs.*

She is not alone. Thousands of good performers each day make similar mistakes. By product selling, they make their jobs tougher than they need to be. Like the salesperson in this example, many salespeople are not aware of how they sell and are not in control of the process. It's not that what they are doing is wrong; there is simply a better way. When challenged by a client, most salespeople become defensive. When salespeople fear they will get shut out by an objection, most start to push—themselves and their product—even if their tone remains friendly. Many intend to be consultative—need-based sellers; many *think* they are. Some salespeople do get adversarial. For example, one cash management banker from a top bank responded to a customer who griped about a better offer, "Well, if you don't care about quality, go with them." What a way to talk to a client! But you don't have to become defensive or adversarial. Instead of trying to think of how you can rebut, *listen, listen, listen.* Scan for key words, which you can penetrate to learn more. Take notes, show empathy, *ask questions.* Our "take it or leave it" banker would have faired a lot better had he inquired about the "better offer" and made some comparisons: "I can see how you want to get the best pricing.

Salesperson's responses	Skill analyses	Sales problem	Feedback	Consultative approach
"I can understand your being satisfied with your present system."	Empathy	The empathy here is good, but the salesperson made an *assumption* that the client was satisfied with his present system. The client *didn't* say, "I'm satisfied"; he said, "I don't want to change." The salesperson wasn't *really* listening; not really responding to a real objection. The client may have hated his system but didn't want to change for a host of other reasons.	Salesperson should maintain empathy but avoid making assumptions; listen more closely for a key word(s) such as *change*.	"I can understand your concerns about changing." Then ask a question about change.
"But our system is superior."	*But* — the great contradictor. The salesperson is giving a generic response. *But* usually negates what the client just said.	The salesperson used a generic statement that was unsubstantiated at this point; she was insensitive in her disagreement with client. At the very least her comment would have caused the client to feel defensive about his system.	Don't compare your product until you know what you are comparing it to. Ask. Find out!	"May I ask why you feel that way?" or "May I ask what your concerns about changing are?"

Salesperson's responses	Skill analyses	Sales problem	Feedback	Consultative approach
"Can your system address your needs for the future?"	This question was designed to get client to see he hadn't thought about the future.	This is a closed-end question. But *more* important, the salesperson failed to find out what the client's needs were. The salesperson was looking for a problem *before* she understood the situation. A better progression is situation, problem, need, not the other way around. In addition to this, the salesperson risked offending the client or conveying a possible threatening tone at this early stage of call.	Use an open-ended question to find out what the client's concerns are, what is going on, and what the client needs.	"To see if we can add value, may I ask how does your system work?" "What needs do you anticipate for the future?"

Proposals in our field can be very different. May I ask what's included in their proposal so we can compare them for scope, value, and, of course, price?" Once you get into the client's thinking, you can *position* your idea or product. It isn't the words in the above example that are important; it's *how the salesperson thought about the selling process.*

Summary of the Six Critical Skills

The six critical skills—presence, relating, questioning, listening, positioning, checking, are the heart of consultative selling. Clients today are not blank slates. Don't try to educate them. Instead, think in terms of *learning with* them and *helping* them. Salespeople aren't blank slates either. You as a salesperson know how to sell—no one can teach you to sell. But your *awareness* of what you know you do and of what you don't do can be increased and your level of performance will be increased along with it. To reach the next level you have to know what to do more of, what to do less of, and what to change. Let's look in depth at what needs to happen in each of the six elements of the framework and then at the six critical skills to help you master this process and polish your present skills—to reach the next level of performance.

PART 1

The Six Critical Elements of the Framework

1
Framework: Opening

In selling there is a simple rule: "Give before you get." Without a doubt the opening is the time and place for you to begin to give — to earn the right to get. On the phone, the time to give is usually abbreviated, compared to face-to-face selling. *Everything becomes condensed over the phone.* The amount of time normally available to open in a face-to-face contact (introduce yourself, build rapport, establish your purpose, and so on) is usually not there for phone calls. The 15 minutes you might get in a face-to-face call frequently dwindles down to 1 to 3 minutes or fewer over the phone.

Because time gets compressed on the phone and because it is much easier for the client to say no or disengage, an effective and natural opening is very important. A good opening requires that you have an *agenda* and a *clear focus* of what you want to achieve *before* you make the call. You must ask yourself, "What do I want out of this call?" and "What's in it for the client?" Before you pick up the telephone, ask yourself, "Why should this client listen to me?" A present client can easily get off the line by saying, "Joe, sorry, I have another call," or a prospect can say, "Listen, I'm not interested," and hang up. You may face obstacles in trying to get to your client or prospect through a "gatekeeper" such as the secretary. Since just getting through to your contact can be a challenge, it is foolhardy not to be prepared to maximize the moment once you get through. *Remember you are selling, not just calling.*

Opening with clients or prospects you haven't met face to face is usually more difficult than opening with someone with whom you already have rapport. One face-to-face meeting (replete with eye contact, a hand shake, and rapport) usually helps "pre-personalize" a telephone situation. Attaching a face to your voice makes most clients more receptive to your calls and ideas. For this reason, most telephone salespeople engaged in large or complex sales meet their prospects and clients *early* in the relationship—within the first or second month—to add a human dimension. Of course, many telephone selling situations cannot include a face-to-face meeting for economical or practical reasons—for example with smaller clients or under time pressures. This is especially true in a blanket prospecting effort, where the objective is to reach a large number of prospects for a small ticket item. But even in these situations, successful telephone salespeople know that they have extra work in store for them to compensate for not having had a handshake.

The opening is the time to establish rapport and create a focus for the call. However, because time is limited, you must develop a strong sense of how much leeway you have for pleasantries or chitchat. This will depend of course on many factors, including your relationship, the client, the situation, your objective for the call, and the time of day, but normally time for chatting is less than time in face-to-face situations (especially in calls to prospects you don't know). Often you can chat for only a few moments—even seconds. This is particularly true when in addition to client resistance you have restrictions on *your* time. For example, an institutional salesperson may need to complete early morning calls to key clients, or may be calling under a project deadline or to reach clients before other salespeople do. Some telephone salespeople have time-per-call restrictions. But even with time restrictions, rapport is still a key element. Rapport isn't only a function of chitchat; rapport is created as much by an up, friendly voice and positive, caring words ("*Good* morning, how are *you* today?"), confidence (which conveys you have something of value), and a focused approach so as *not to waste your client's time*. Certainly a hinge (connection with the individual you are calling) helps enormously in your opening to establish rapport (see Part 4).

Since the telephone does not allow for eye contact, your voice and words create a presence and say, "I'm positive, prepared, focused, worth listening to." Your voice bears a great deal of the burden for building rapport. A bad attitude, a disinterested tone, a sign of impatience, a vague, fuzzy statement of purpose—all these are easy to read and are guaranteed to destroy the rapport and credibility you need to get started.

It takes skill, discipline, and an appreciation for how important rapport is to make sure that your tone remains positive and that you don't become impatient or frustrated after a long series of calls. For example, since prospects are usually not expecting your call, they may miss your name or your company's name, and you may have to repeat and spell both countless times. You may have to explain who you are and why you are calling over and over and over. The prospect may also ask how you got his or her name. You may be having a hectic day filled with interruptions or deadlines. If exasperation or impatience comes through in your voice, your chances for success will fade fast! You may have to call back six times. If you feel you are losing your patience, take a few deep breaths, stay off the telephone for a few minutes while you regroup, and go over the six critical skills.

But, as important as it is, rapport is only one aspect of the opening. A great deal more has to be achieved in the opening before getting into needs and ideas, and it has to be accomplished relatively *fast* on the phone. First you need to show the clients *what's in it for them,* so they stay on the line. Let's look at all the components of the opening: greeting and introduction, rapport, summary, hinge, purpose (potential benefits to clients), and bridge to needs.

Greeting/Introduction

Your greeting creates the first impression, and it should be professional, natural, and welcoming: A simple good morning or good afternoon is a good way to start. *Use the client's name,* whether it is the first name or Mr., Ms., or Mrs. as appropriate. Next, with a prospect, say your name, as well as your organization, and possibly tell one sentence or so to emphasize what about your organization should interest the prospect. Say, "This is X with . . . organization in the Y group dedicated to (benefit to client)."

If you are trying to get through a gatekeeper, say, "This is X. May I speak with John Smith?" (See Part 4 for details on getting through gatekeepers.) Whether you use your client's or prospect's first name or Mr. or Ms. depends on the relationship, situation, and what is accepted in your industry or area. When there is the slightest doubt, opt for the more formal approach and *wait* for the client to offer you his or her first name. Asking, "May I call you Paul?" in the first few seconds is not appropriate. Clients who do not suggest a first-name basis may be signaling that they want a more formal approach with you. If this formality continues through a call, the client may just be very formal, or the formality could be a signal that you have not gotten very far on the rapport curve. Government representatives, top executives, doctors, and members of the clergy should be called Mr., Ms., Dr., or Rev. unless they clearly indicate otherwise.

In a first call, as you introduce yourself, leverage what you have—whether it is a referral or being a full service firm or a specialty one. In a clear, confident way tell who you are, what you do, and what you represent. It is foolish to make any first call (or any call in which you expect difficulty getting through) without doing some homework. Leverage another relationship ("X in our firm . . . "), someone outside your firm ("X mentioned to me . . . "), or any information you get beforehand that helps get you through and shows that you took the time to learn something *before* you picked up the telephone. Unless there is no choice, don't call "hard" cold. The last thing you want to hear if you are a bond salesperson is, "Hey, we don't do bonds. What are you calling me for?" Do your homework, or your lack of preparation not only will kill rapport, it will close down communications.

Just a word about the opening when you are the recipient of the call. How your firm (secretary or receptionist) greets incoming callers is very important. They are the first line of communication, and their approach should convey to callers that they have reached a professional and focused organization. Every salesperson should call his or her own line periodically to check how it is being answered. The opening should be professional and standard (yes, standard, like the precise moves of a gymnast). How the telephones are answered reflect the culture of the organization as much as anything else!

Rapport

From the first moment, it is important to project confidence *without sounding arrogant* or pushy. The real problem with arrogance, apart from turning clients off, is that it is usually accompanied by complacency and a lack of imagination and innovation. If you keep in mind that your intent is to be *helpful,* you can build rapport with people you don't know in a genuine way.

Even when time is limited, take a few seconds to establish rapport with your prospect, client or gatekeeper. This could range from a simple "George, how are you doing?" to a customer or "Hello, how are you today?" to a prospect, to a more formal, "I appreciate speaking with you"; what you say should take into account cultural and regional factors. Even when the client or prospect does not respond in kind with a friendly tone or comment, you will have lost nothing and actually have gained something — insight into how difficult and guarded the client may be.

There are hundreds of ways to build rapport, and not all of them center on talking about things such as Little League. Many top telephone salespeople say that, until they know the client, at least a little, they do not engage in chitchat because it would seem ingenuine. Many wait until the end of the phone call, a number of calls later, or after a face-to-face meeting to develop the basis for personal chitchat. There are many ways to establish rapport, from small things such as thanking clients at the end of the call for their time or remembering to thank the client for having met with you the day before ("Thanks again for your time") to being sensitive to the client's comments or needs or reading a voice that sounds distracted.

Rapport is as important with inbound calls from clients as it is with the outbound calls you make. With inbound calls, clients are at least interested in speaking with someone, even if they are only calling to complain. But a lack of rapport building and interest from a salesperson can kill any client's goodwill and most certainly will further aggravate an unhappy client. One salesperson with a well-known mutual fund destroyed rapport with the way he answered an incoming call from a prospect. The prospect was referred to him, by name, by an executive with a major corporation. The prospect made the call to the salesperson at 3:30 p.m. on a Friday afternoon in June to request information on a mutual fund. The salesperson (or should I say the order-taker), without asking any questions to uncover needs, term, amount or investment philosophy, took the information volunteered by the prospect. The salesperson's voice was flat and disinterested. He actually sounded annoyed. While he promptly sent information to the prospect, he did not bother to attach a personal note, letter, or business card. The packaging was unprofessional—a 5-inch-thick stack prospectus bound by a soiled, fat rubber band. He did not follow up.

The salesperson's failure to even attempt to break the ice was the tip of a no-win iceberg, and it equaled a giant sales freeze-out. His three minutes of telephone time lost him a sale and cost him and his firm a long-term client. The loss of this prospect would be significant in the bull market environment current at that time, but it became more significant in the bear market soon to follow. This truly was "rubberband marketing"—marketing at its worst.

Of course, there will be occasions when you will curtail your icebreaking effort because of *signals* from the client or prospect. For example, if the clients say they are tight for time, if their voices read cold, or if you are making a series of calls to the same person in one day, jump to the quick: "Don, on the wire, we are seeing . . . " or "Don, how . . . " Also, in calls to brand-new prospects, you can appropriately limit the rapport to, "Hello, how are you today?" and a positive tone of voice. Then, based on the response, you can decide if a moment of chitchat is appropriate.

Transition

Although time spent on rapport is time well spent, if you find yourself with a chatty client with whom the chitchat seems to be going on too long, you can *control* the situation. Wait for the client to take a breath and move on to your next point. For example, you could summarize your last contact ("Well, as we talked about last Tuesday, I thought I'd . . . "), refer to your purpose ("Well, I am calling about . . . "), or ask a question related to your purpose ("You know, I was thinking of . . . What do you think?") or "That leads to . . . ", even if it doesn't really lead to your topic. Comments as brief as these can transition the chitchat into a business discussion.

Many salespeople are concerned that once they embark on rapport, they won't be able to get "back" to business. But rapport is a part of business. Spending too much time on rapport isn't normally a problem with selling, especially to prospects on the telephone. As a matter of fact, the problem is quite the opposite. When you are calling someone you don't know, the situation can be downright cold.

Hinge

An effective way to warm up your opening to a prospect or to interest a present client is by using a hinge. A hinge is a means you can use to connect with your client from a personal referral to research on the company. For example, you can use a personal referral ("I am calling at the suggestion of . . . ") or you can use research ("I read about X . . . Congratulations . . . to see how we might . . . "). With a present client you could use a topic not directly related to your business reason for calling as your hinge, such as a conference you and the client will be attending or tickets to a concert.

Agenda/Objective/Purpose

Fairly quickly with present clients but especially with prospects, in the opening you need to tell the client why you are calling. You need to briefly set your agenda by saying *why* you are calling and then, equally quickly, because clients can disengage so easily, listing the potential benefits to the client, clearly telling *why* the client should listen and talk to you. As you set your agenda for your telephone call, define your *objective* and *purpose* before you pick up the telephone. Your objective is what you want to get out of the call. The more measurable and specific your objective, the better it will help you focus the call. Your *purpose* is the flip side of your objective and tells the client, *"What's in it for you?"* For example, you could say, "To speak with you about . . . we see a way that *could* very likely reduce your exposure . . . " or "reduce fees. . . . " Such *potential* benefits should be presented early in the opening or you may find yourself disconnected. In addition, you can create an agenda to help you organize the topics you plan to cover. If you are new to telephone selling, it is invaluable to have a written agenda in front of you as you call — and take notes on it. Since it is so easy to forget things over the telephone and to make mistakes because things are rushed, a written agenda is indispensable. It also provides an excellent format for taking notes.

Objectives come in all sizes, including getting the prospect to agree to accept a second call from you (you definitely don't want to hear, "Don't call me again!"), getting an appointment, or closing an order on the phone. To maintain your credibility, don't make exaggerated claims. By positioning your purpose as a *potential* benefit, you can avoid overstating what you can do. Clients recoil from exaggerated claims and often respond in a challenging and hostile way to them. Since how your client responds to your purpose will determine how long you get to stay on the line, it is critical to know how to get a dialogue going. For example, if you are calling a CFO at the suggestion of her or his insurance broker to set an appointment to arrange to have him or her visit your home or office, instead of saying, "We can save you millions of dollars . . . " say, "Barbara, we'd like to set a time for you, X risk manager, and Y broker to come out and visit with us to get to know one another more and to see how we *could* possibly work with you to improve your insurance program. We think we see ways to *significantly* lower the costs of . . . " Setting an objective, purpose, and knowing the agenda items you want to cover before you call are crucial. The clearer the objectives are, the more likely you'll reach them.

Time Check

In some situations, if you plan to do much more than ask for an appointment and, especially with prospects, you have stated a potential benefit (your purpose), *you can ask the client if it is a good time to talk.* This is optional depending on your objective, relationship, and market. It is a small gesture of courtesy and an additional way to establish rapport which is often appreciated by the client and gives him or her a moment to react. You are counting on the strength of your purpose (what's in it for the client). When clients say they don't have time to talk, you can use your judgment and either deal with it as an objection or set a time to call the client back. Of course, when you finally get to prospects or clients who are difficult to reach or who are likely to say they don't have time just as a way to get off the line, forgo the time check and go for it!

Bridge to Needs

Once you have successfully greeted the client, introduced yourself, established rapport, etc., you may think you are ready to start selling. And you are, but remember, selling is not only talking. It is listening first! *Before you begin to present any ideas or*

*features and benefits at any level of detail, you should get informa-
tion from the client.* Discipline yourself to detour from product.
Go to needs before product.

Let's look at an uncomplicated telephone sale. You are calling
Ms. Ellen Smith to sell her a gold card. She is a priority prospect,
a second-year medical student. After you state your objective, *before* you get to your purpose (you have been on the telephone less
than one minute), she objects: "I already have a card." If you are
very new to sales, you might disengage—a clear mistake. But if
you respond like 29 out of 30 salespeople, you would begin to
present benefits, saying, "Well let me just tell you about . . . we
offer service . . . 365 days a year . . . " or "We provide X dollars
of free insurance . . . travel . . . air tickets . . . " or any one of a
dozen other benefits. But frankly, in most situations, you might
as well hang up. The odds are Ms. Smith would not be swayed.
Why? Because she would feel a product push coming and put up
her defenses.

Most salespeople sell products. Again, they may not intend to,
but they do. Whether salespeople are selling a gold card, a swap,
or a pharmaceutical product to a buying group for 100 hospitals,
whether the sale is $10 or $10 million, many give generic answers
to generic objections, by rattling off features and benefits equally
and often unimpressively. The alternative to dumping is entering
a *flow* with the client. But this takes know-how; more specifically,
this takes questioning and listening.

If there is one place where the risk of a salesperson doing a
product dump is greatest, it is right after the opening of the telephone call. It takes discipline not to jump into product. The ten-
dency for salespeople is to present. The alternative is to *position,*
which requires identifying needs first. Selling is to talking what
modern dance is to walking—selling takes discipline, flexibility,
and practice. The opening is where your craft meets its first hard
test. The opening allows you to "give" through your greeting,
introduction, summary, hinge, objective, and purpose. Only
then, once you give, are you in a position to begin to get—get
information so you can talk about something meaningful to the
client.

It is interesting to note that many salespeople aren't aware of
the moment when the opening is over. Actually, recognizing this

point is significant because it means going somewhere: product or needs. Awareness and skill will determine where you go. Without really being aware that is what they are doing, many salespeople go to product — too soon. When the client starts talking about his or her situation or you talk about your product or when needs are being discussed, you are out of the opening phase of the sale. If you are talking about a product at that point before understanding needs, you may be doing a product dump. Our credit card salesperson may have done better with: "Yes. I can appreciate you already have a card (empathy). To see if there are any benefits such as free insurance (brief commercial) we can offer to you, *may I ask which card you currently have?*" The objective would be to find out what services the client lacks. For example, if the client had a card that required full payment each month, the salesperson would have a possible in with minimum payments.

Regardless of what you are selling, asking allows you to position what you say about your product. Questions will also help reduce your clients' defensiveness by showing you are interested in their situations. People expect salespeople to make a pitch, but good "why" questions say to clients that you want to understand their needs to see if you can offer something of value. In a sense, questions disarm the client who otherwise will be turned off by a canned pitch, but more importantly, questions let you understand how the client thinks and allow you to shape and craft how you talk about your product so there is a match up between product and needs. The most compelling reason to train yourself to ask questions is that questions will help you sell by giving you information. One salesperson was able to turn a no into something else when his customer said no. Instead of ignoring the no and reciting a list of other offerings or giving up/taking no for an answer, he asked why. He learned about a possible acquisition and introduced his investment banking people, who eventually won the business from the company's traditional investment bank.

Objections Up Front

Before leaving the topic of the opening, we should discuss objections briefly, because regardless of how effectively you open, telephone clients are apt to object, even more than they would in face-to-face situations. It is just easier to say no over the telephone. Objections, especially from prospects, are a natural reaction — a form of self-protection. To avoid hearing a pitch or having to make a decision, clients and prospects will put up smoke screens early! Like the old song, "You Always Hurt the One You Love," clients are just as likely — if not more likely — to object if they are interested as if they are not interested. Typical "natural" objections that are often put up as a smoke screen are, "I'm really busy right now," "I'm already covered," "I have too many . . . ," "I'm not interested," "I don't need it," "I don't want to change," "I just bought it," "I'm satisfied with X," "I don't have time," "I don't want it," "I don't have any money," "I don't like it," "I already have one."

Objections are a vital part of the sales process. Expect them and appreciate them. They identify barriers and put a spotlight on them. They help the sales process by providing you with a way to gain credibility *if* you can deal with them. Objections are a problem only when you can't deal with them. Of course, some objections are insurmountable, but many can be dealt with; although no product or organization is perfect, often one aspect can compensate for another.

Almost all objections have been heard before, especially opening smoke screen objections. Therefore, you can anticipate them and prepare for them. Sales organizations should give rewards to salespeople who hear and bring in *new* objections, since such information can be used to prepare the entire sales force. For example, if you work for a bank that is recognized in the retail banking area but is not perceived as strong in commercial banking, you can expect to hear early on in the call, "I thought you were a retail bank." Unless you are ready to resolve this objection, you will get shut out *fast*. Similarly, a commercial bank moving into the investment banking arena should be ready for, "I have a relationship with an investment bank," "You don't have a track record," "I'm concerned about execution," or "Stick to the credit side." If a firm has had bad press in the Sunday paper, the sales force can expect comments like, "I'm concerned . . . ," "What's happening with . . . ?"

If you can't deal with the wave of objections up front, you will lose opportunities because it is so easy for clients to get off the telephone. While we will cover objections in depth in Chap. 4, keep in mind that like rejection, objections come with the territory in telephone selling — especially as you open with prospects on the phone. So be ready for them in the opening. In most situations be prepared to give at least a second and possibly a third effort before hanging up — for now. Except in extreme cases (generally when the prospect does not qualify) don't give up without at *least* a second effort. (See Part 4.)

Looking Ahead to "Presence"

Although presence is one of the six critical skills discussed in Chap. 7, it is so important to a successful opening that we should look at it before moving on to the next phase. This vital factor is hard to describe but easy to spot. In telephone situations, it is your voice first and foremost that tells how confident and comfortable you feel. When you don't feel "right" in these ways, it will likely come through in your voice. Therefore, it is helpful to practice, listen to yourself, tape yourself to hear how you sound and to increase your comfort level. If you are new to selling, if necessary, write out your opening (but don't read it verbatim or it will sound stale and canned) and practice talking it out in different ways, using the client's name. Since mispronunciation of difficult names sets things off poorly and is usually the *first* sign of a "telemarketer" versus a business contact, this could be a critical element. If necessary, do some research, such as confirming with the secretary or third party how to pronounce names correctly. If you are calling someone for the first time, say all difficult names to yourself two times before you pick up the telephone: "Bill Windeshammer," "Mr. Windeshammer. . . . " If you get caught off guard once and communicate a lack of knowledge and confidence because of an unanticipated question, learn from that experience and be ready for the situation next time. For example, if you were on the trading floor, and you stumbled and stammered when your trader asked you for your thoughts on what the market will do, be ready the next time to at least describe market "flavor."

New salespeople in particular need to think through how they will open to make sure they don't undermine their chances for success. Your voice, your diction, pace, word choice, all "speak" for you. Enunciate clearly, don't rush but don't drag it out either. Your pace is indicative of your level of comfort. Your choice of words, coupled with clear and well-paced speech, can communicate interest and confidence. Eliminate words such as *just* in comments such as, "I've *just* been here *two months.*" Never talk your products down, as in, "It's not important . . . " or "You probably wouldn't be interested, but . . . " since they minimize the importance of why you are calling and set a negative tone. As one successful broker says, "You can't say yes for a customer, so don't say no. Be optimistic." Avoid slang, informal or casual speech. Treat the client as someone special. Make your presentation clear, articulate, and friendly but professional and genuine.

Summary of Opening

In summary, the opening accomplishes:

- Greeting and introduction
- Summary/hinge (referral)
- Objective/purpose/agenda
- Time check (optional)
- Bridge to needs

The confidence and tone you project in the opening are very important. The ability to deal with objections in the opening is also important. The opening is more than saying hello, it is the initial few minutes you get to establish who you are, what your agenda is, and why the client should participate in the call. The short time opening takes is disproportionate to how much impact an opening has on what happens next! Be ready to maximize it.

2
Framework:
Client Needs

Where do most salespeople go in the sales process after they open? Most go directly to product. They may not intend to, but many jump into a monologue presentation before they know the lay of the land. And they pay a hefty price for doing so. An alternative, and one that is all too often missed, is to ask questions to identify or confirm needs *first*. An effective opening has earned you the right to do this.

Take the time to identify or confirm needs so that you can focus your sales discussion and position your products. In your opening you will have given, and, therefore, you will have *paved* the way to "get." You can get needs as well as information to determine if the client qualifies. Don't begin to talk about your product or idea *before* you bring the client into the discussion. *Listen before you tell.* Most salespeople fail to do this. One salesperson took a call from a client who called on his 800 number to find out about mutual funds. He said that he had a $25,000 certificate of deposit (CD) coming due. Rather than asking a qualifying question—finding out something about the prospect's needs, or even when the CD was coming due—this salesperson (possibly driven by a 2- or 3-minute time limit) said, "I will send you information on our X fund and a copy of our magazine" and hung up. Not surprisingly, the client, sitting with the newspaper in front of him, called another 800 number! Although this salesperson may have met his time objective, he failed to meet his ultimate objective — selling mutual funds. He would have engaged his client more fully with a comment like, "Thank you for calling us. Certainly we have. . . . May I ask a few questions to make sure we send . . . ?" and "When will your CD mature?"

But salespeople are not the only culprits who create a product dump. Clients often invite — even insist — on one. They may say, "What do you have for me today?" or "Tell me what you can do." Savvy salespeople recognize this for the trap that it is — a fast way for the client to avoid buying anything. The key is to *give* but not to dump. For example, you might say, "I read about X . . . (or I've been interested to meet with you. . . . We have . . . Our commitment to . . . We are seeing . . .)". The key is to "give" for a *few minutes* (1 to 3) *at most* and then to *check,* "How does that sound so far? How does that fit in with your situation?" or "To help me focus, what . . . ?"

Many clients who seem to put up "initial" road blocks by asking for product information, holding back answers, or giving very general ones are often more than willing to answer such questions once you have laid out one or two ideas. *The key is to check with them and not proceed to a product dump.* They may have held back because you haven't yet earned your stripes. Maybe your opening didn't warrant more of an exchange, or your question was not clear and confident enough. It could be that the client simply wasn't comfortable with you or expected to listen first and then decide. In facing situations like these, many salespeople begin hawking their wares. When you have asked a question and gotten little or no information, you can try asking a good back-up question or you can begin to give *some* information. Remember, however, after talking for about three minutes to check and ask for feedback. For example, you could ask, "How does that sound, Ann?" Most clients, especially if things don't exactly match up, will respond and provide you with information they wouldn't or couldn't give earlier that you can use to position your ideas.

When asked why they don't ask questions before discussing product, salespeople offer a wide array of reasons. The two main reasons are that (1) questions will cost them too much valuable time or (2) they will lose control. Although it is true that there is less time on the phone than there is in face-to-face selling situations, each sliver of time must be valued all the more. But even when questions extend a call slightly, the quality of the call is usually improved. In fact, good questions can even shorten a call by helping focus it. If you can encourage your clients to tell you their needs or concerns, you will be able to hone in on a particular product or capability that matches up with those needs more quickly.

The alternative to asking need questions is just to assume that the benefits you want to present are a match with the client's needs and to plunge into a presentation. But product selling frequently short-circuits because, even if you are presenting the right product or idea, you may be presenting it from the wrong perspective. If you are off the mark and proceed in that vein you will lose your client's interest fast, waste time, and miss opportunities. By diving directly into a product discussion without finding needs and getting feedback, you risk shutting off the conversation. Even if your idea is a match, today's clients respond better if you check with them, since this says to the clients that your approach is not going to be hard sell. When you talk about your clients' needs and situations, you motivate them to listen and buy. Client needs are the best path to closing sales.

Plunging into the product without bothering to identify or check needs looks and feels like you are pushing a product, not satisfying your client needs. Also, it is presumptuous for you to think you have all the answers without asking the questions. You can't divine client needs, and you shouldn't trivialize clients by suggesting their needs are like everyone else's. You can't read their minds. If you think you don't need to ask questions, you are probably making a costly mistake.

Homework is essential in understanding client needs, but it cannot replace asking questions and listening to answers. You need both homework and questions to enable you to understand your clients' needs and to differentiate your products. Your planned questions will help you get at key chunks of information. They also lead you to spontaneous questions which will help you capitalize on general information you uncover. Questioning enables you to create a dialogue and avoid the common and easily detected "script" approach to telephone selling. The most obvious script is the written script that is read to the client. But some salespeople who don't physically use scripts use them mentally. *They tell the same story to everyone.* But there are simply too many salespeople calling the same clients for anyone to do this successfully. In today's competitive sales environment filled with sophisticated clients and look-alike products, you need to tailor how you talk to your clients or you will sound like everyone else. (See Chap. 9 for in-depth information on questioning skills.)

3
Framework: Positioning Product/Idea

Positioning is in today; presenting is out. *Presenting* is telling your story *from your or your company's point of view. Positioning* is telling your story from *your client's point of view.* Positioning is the "superskill" because it is the end product of questioning and listening. Since we are in a client generation, positioning helps you put the focus where it should be—on the client. But in order to position, you *must* know the client's story, situation, and needs.

Knowing the needs of the client is the heart of consultative selling. One of the true advantages of consultative selling is that it allows you to differentiate your product. The process of positioning helps you discuss your products in the context of what your client needs. One of the best ways to differentiate your products from their look-alike contenders is to position your product as a solution by matching it up with the client's needs and separating you and your product from the pack.

It is much more effective to be able to say to a client, "You mentioned . . . concern about . . . swaps . . . I have a computer program that can analyze . . . to give you that information . . . and since we are number one in swaps, we would (benefit) . . . " rather than to tell a generic story such as "We are number one in swaps." Although you should capitalize on being number one, keep in mind your number-one status has meaning only in so far as it benefits the client.

The main challenge that salespeople face today is that most clients and even some salespeople think products are generic. Salespeople who can differentiate their products have an edge. The generic product syndrome is the sales challenge of the nineties, and because of it product differentiation has become a major issue. The old tried and true "present features and benefits" doesn't go far enough. The features and benefits of competing products often look too much alike—and sometimes *are* too much alike—at least on the surface (sometimes even upon closer inspection) to warrant reliance on product-based selling. Even companies that lead the market in introducing new products and product innovations face the same problem because competitors catch up so fast.

The need to know how to position doesn't diminish the importance of having competitive products or knowing your products. In today's competitive world, these are a given. But today you need to talk about the client's situation as much or more than you talk about your products. Today you must expand your definition of features and benefits to go beyond core features and benefits to value-added ones.

Core features are the characteristics that make up a product—things like fixed rate or the compounds or research behind a pharmaceutical product. Core benefits are the value or reward derived from the core features, such as stability, reducing risk, peace of mind, savings, protection for one's family, convenience, and safety.

Value-added features and benefits go beyond what you put directly into the product; they describe the benefits of working with you and your organization. Both core and value-added features and benefits are needed today to differentiate. Some salespeople talk features, features, and more features. But clients buy client benefits. One company's salesforce stressed to its clients that its data retrieval system was the best in the industry. Yet sales were not going as anticipated. Finally, upon examination of that data retrieval system, they finally found only one client benefit, speed of contracts. Clients were nonplussed when the retrieval system was discussed, but those with short time frames livened up when they heard about getting their contracts more quickly. As you sell, you need to do more than link features and benefits. You must verbally (and in letters and proposals) weave features and benefits with client needs. Features give the credibility, benefits give the marketability, *but positioning makes the sale. Tailored benefits drive features home by telling the clients what's in it for them.* In the past, features made up half of the language of sales and benefits the other half. Today, the proportions are one-third features, one-third benefits, and one-third client needs. Positioning enables you to "translate" your product into the client's language.

A decade ago or less, core features and benefits (products themselves) were the differentiators. Today differentiation is achieved through *value-added* (client-related) features and benefits—what you and your organization bring to the table that is special to the particular client. The successful salesperson brings up not only tangibles but intangibles such as track record, quality, service, ability to execute, the skill level of professionals, commitment, and reputation. To differentiate your product you should capitalize on *all* your features and benefits, core and value-added. The combined total of your core and value-added features and benefits make up your *total offer.* That total offer, matched up with what the client needs, composes your real "product." Products no longer can be separated from product fit. And how you talk about your products will vary from client to client—the conservative buyer will like the tradition of your firm and your old school ties, while the entrepreneur wants to know you can get the deal done fast!

In short, *today the product is the equalizer, and you, your organization, and how well you can craft a product story are the differentiator.* You must draw on all your resources, use your total offer—why you, what's special about your organization and you, and what's special about your client—and position accordingly.

4

Framework: Objections and Resolutions of Objections

Because it is easier for clients on the telephone to say no, be rude, or disengage more easily than in face-to-face selling situations, being able to resolve objections in telephone selling is essential. In sales seminars, every time we ask salespeople what they want to work on, objections appear at the top of their list. Objections are an integral part of the telephone selling process. Objections at least show you that your client is listening. Objections can be a knee-jerk reaction, the way clients protect themselves and guard their time and money, as much as they are an expression of real concern.

Clients object for countless reasons — from being angry, to genuinely misunderstanding, to wanting to protect themselves, to being obstinate, to testing you. But in almost all situations, objections are a sign the client needs more information. Regardless of the reason for each objection, every objection needs to be resolved or off-set before a deal can be closed. An attitude of respect for the client — one in which you appreciate that most clients truly know more about their needs than you do — is the first step in resolving objections. Salespeople who genuinely *respect* their clients have a natural edge. The objection resolution process we will discuss in this section will give them another edge. At the other extreme, salespeople who disdain their clients and don't know how to sell to the client of the nineties eventually will lose them. Additionally, you need good, solid product, market, and client information to deal with objections. Finally, you will need to be persistent and patient. But as important as all these elements are, you will also need skills — six of them (presence, relating, questioning, listening, positioning, checking).

Almost all salespeople can feel frustrated when clients object. Being able to resolve objections is the acid test for every salesperson, because in order to effectively deal with objections in a helpful and persuasive way (by helping customers to be open to listening and helping them convince themselves), all six critical skills come into play. Objections, however, are far from the end of the sales opportunity. They can be the beginning — a chance to get to the nitty gritty, build credibility, and gain ground. Objections indicate to you that the client is listening, considering your idea, and sparring with it, possibly because he or she is attracted to it. Persistence is an important attribute for salespeople, especially in telephone sales. Since objections can be a natural reaction, usually a second and third effort are appropriate to resolve each objection. Of course, you have to develop a sense of when to back off so that you don't provoke the client. Sometimes one effort at resolving an objection may be enough, but this is rare in telephone selling. The salesperson from a different branch, for instance, who unknowingly calls someone who is already a client of the firm needs to know how to handle this "prospect" who says, "I already deal with your firm! Don't you guys know what you are doing?" The salesperson needs to know how to quickly and gracefully exit with a "Well, I very much appreciate your telling me about this. It's good to hear you are a client here. We have different divisions. . . . May I ask who you deal with? Great . . . I'll let him . . . How . . . thank you."

But unlike this situation, a second and third effort is *usually* warranted. Persistence does not and should not be synonymous with hard sell. For example, if a prospect says, "It doesn't fit us," "I don't need it," or "I'm not interested," many salespeople resort to a product dump, believing they are being need-oriented. But instead of being consultative, they either try to change the client's mind by contradicting the client or they virtually ignore the objection and press on. An alternative to this is to use the *objection resolution model*. The model gives you a *process* (not a script) which you can use to help resolve objections without the wear-and-tear of a hard sell. Let's examine how each of the six critical skills can be used to resolve objections.

The objection resolution model consists of five parts: presence, empathy, questioning, position, check.

Presence. When clients object it is important for you to maintain your presence and project concern and confidence without appearing crestfallen. If a client is aggressive in a face-to-face situation, you can move your body back a bit to give the client room but inch up in your chair and straighten your spine to show your confidence. Over the telephone, you must use your voice and silences to communicate confidence and give your client room. Even if your nemesis is mentioned, you can remain confident. As clients object, stay patient and listen. *Don't interrupt.* Don't show signs of impatience or defensiveness. Don't convey arrogance or hostility. And although objections are expressed to you personally, they are not usually directed at you personally, so don't take them personally. Look at each objection as a spotlight on a problem. Use your knowledge and the consultative sales process to solve the problem. Most objections—when you take the emotions out of them—are no more than requests for more information. Trust the objection resolution process and use it.

Empathy. Show *empathy* to relate to your clients. Tell them with words and tone that you are interested in and open to their point of view. When clients object, they are in a negative mode. Empathy from you can help defuse any negative feelings they have. Empathy from you says, "I care. I'm open." Empathy does not mean you agree; it means you are open to listening. Sometimes your own agenda can get in the way of empathizing with clients. For example, one young salesperson barely listened when his client told him, "It's not a good time to talk. My wife just called. My daughter has left college." The young man replied, "Oh, don't worry. She's a smart kid. She'll be alright. She'll go back. I was calling about . . . " Needless to say, he didn't make his sale. More important, he lost long-term relationship points.

The process of empathy followed by a question is straightforward. It is simple, but it is not easy. This point was driven home to me when I asked a class of 60 MBAs I was teaching at an Ivy League school to respond with empathy to a client objection. It took a while before they could develop a personalized, genuine, empathy statement.

The class exercise was as follows: Students were told to play the role of an investment banking analyst. They were to imagine themselves in a meeting where the CFO of a bank about to be acquired said, "Those numbers are too low." They were asked to come up with a response.

There was a precedent for this case in real life which I related to them. A young analyst was in a meeting with a CFO who complained about low numbers. The young man's boss, a managing director of his firm, hearing this, turned to his analyst and said, "Explain the numbers." The analyst, half the age of the CFO, who felt uncomfortable addressing the CFO by his first name, responded, "No, Mike, they are right." The CFO responded by shrugging his shoulders. Not surprisingly, this deal fell apart a few weeks later since in matters like M&A, the personal chemistry can be as important as or more important than the numbers. The students were told that the analyst's response was inappropriate.

I asked the students to develop an alternative response, but at first they could not. Their efforts made it clear that empathy does not come easily and neither do questions. Most of the students (more than half of whom had sales backgrounds prior to coming to business school) felt that giving a detailed *explanation* of how the numbers were derived and explaining to the client directly why the numbers were right was the best solution. I kept pressing for empathy and questioning. In a moment of humor and despair the group realized we were stuck. Finally, a student volunteered a "I can understand your concern," which was "technically" an empathy statement but one which I rejected as a "slug." "Dig inside and find *your* empathy," I pushed. Finally one student said, *"Like you, we want to use the best numbers. May I ask you to tell us why you feel the numbers are wrong?"* Eureka—empathy and a question! The class burst into applause. We had discovered empathy and a great question. Prior to this, the students were so fixed on being right, they ignored the task of trying to resolve the client's objection.

Salespeople who view clients as adversarial or think discussions must be win-lose find it difficult to muster up empathy or questions. Even a comment from a client that seems blatantly hostile and adversarial may really represent a lack of knowledge on the client's part. But the only way to find out is by asking questions to find out what is going on. For example, a *Fortune* 500 CEO known as a tough negotiator was buying a jet for his private use. In response to hearing the price over the telephone the CEO said, "That's ridiculous. We have no reason to talk further." Instead of challenging this adversarial client, the sales rep said, "We've done business in the past, and I've really worked on these numbers (empathy). Can you tell me what you are comparing them to that makes you feel this way (question)?" When the CEO began to talk about the weak market for such a plane and oil prices, the sales rep realized the CEO really had no knowledge about the market for used planes and found a way to reopen the discussion—*without* making a concession.

It is very important to know how to show empathy and ask questions. The alternative to doing this is to be *defensive* or to simply give up. While the choice seems clear, from our experience, many, many salespeople do become defensive or just give up. Amazing but true. Why? Because they lack the skills and know-how to respond differently. The image most salespeople recall when they think about selling or "overcoming" objections is one of *telling* and proving they are right by convincing the client. The expression "overcome objections" reflects just that. If you were asked to *overcome* a set of children's blocks assembled on a table, what would you do? Most people would knock the blocks down. If, however, you were asked to *resolve* the set of blocks, you would take a careful look to understand and restructure it. The moral of this analog is simple: Don't overcome objections; understand them, *resolve* them, rebuild the situation.

Sometimes by asking a question you will learn something new that will cause you to change your perspective so that you can move forward. Although the initial objection itself may have absolutely nothing to do with you, *how* you deal with the client's objection will either *provoke* the client further or begin the process of resolving the problem and getting back into flow with the client.

Questioning. Although we discussed questions along with empathy, since they weave so closely in the process, let's look at questioning further. Most objections are vague and broad. Because they are vague, they are almost impossible to satisfy unless specifics are uncovered. Therefore, usually to satisfy the objection (95 percent of the time), you need to ask a question or several questions to narrow it down.

Some salespeople in the process of learning the objection resolution model say they are not sure what questions to ask. Many salespeople ask the wrong ones. Successful questions are *targeted why*-type questions that don't go off on a tangent. The client-focused *why* serves as a "probe" beneath the surface of the objection to find out what is really there. Remember, an objection is only the tip of the iceberg. Objections are typically expressed as a demand or a conclusion. But what you need to know is what brought the client to this point, *why* the client thinks or feels that way, what the need is. *Asking* why does not create the client objection. Asking just gets the objection out and gives you a chance to address it.

Our experience shows that most salespeople just dive in and *try* to answer the objection without asking a question. They either defend their position or give up. In addition, many salespeople who do ask questions ask the wrong questions for the wrong reasons. Be careful not to fall into the trap of asking the *wrong* questions. Let's look at all the things salespeople often do but should *not:*

Don't Ask Questions that Skirt the Issue

CLIENT: "Your service is lousy."

TRADITIONAL SALESPERSON: "What do you look for in service?" (This question goes on a tangent. It is a good question, but it is asked at the wrong time.)

CONSULTATIVE SALESPERSON: "I'm sorry to hear you feel that way. (Show empathy.) I would like to understand your concern and rectify the situation. (Preface.) *May I ask why you say that?* (or, In what way you are not satisfied?)" (Ask *why*.) (Combine empathy, prefacing, and getting to the heart of the concern, then you can get to what they want in regard to service.)

Don't Ask Questions that Insult the Client

CLIENT: "Your price is too high."

TRADITIONAL SALESPERSON: "Well, aren't you interested in quality?" (While you should always connect price and quality, this is *not* the way to do so. This rhetorical question is challenging and confrontational.)

CONSULTATIVE SALESPERSON: "I know you discussed budget constraints. *So that we can compare all factors, can you tell me what you are comparing us to in feeling the price is high?*" (Then once you know what you are being compared to, you can discuss price and value.)

Don't Go from Demand to Demand

CLIENT: "The rate is too low."

TRADITIONAL SALESPERSON: "Well, what rate are you looking for?" (This question goes from one demand to another demand. Use this question much later—before you hang up, for example: "Well at what price will you do it?" This way at least you can get a standing order or parameter and a sense of where the client is.)

CONSULTATIVE SALESPERSON: "Getting a good rate is important. *What are you comparing us to in saying this is too low?*"

Don't Put Words in the Client's Mouth (Use the Client's Words)

CLIENT: "I need flexibility."

TRADITIONAL SALESPERSON: "I know you need to restructure and have the freedom to X." (This presumes what the need for flexibility is. Don't make assumptions or expand the meaning of what the client says — ask!)

CONSULTATIVE SALESPERSON: *"Why is that?"* or *"What is your concern about flexibility?"* (This is an open invitation to get the client to say more.)

Don't Give Up and Don't Blame Someone Else in Your Organization

CLIENT: "Your turn around is too slow."

TRADITIONAL SALESPERSON: "I agree, but there isn't anything I can do." (or "My hands are tied." or *"They . . ."*)

CONSULTATIVE SALESPERSON: "I know timing is important to you. When do you need it. . . . What has led you to think we will be slow? How would it work for you to get X at this time and then . . . "

When you ask a question, make it one that "enters" the heart of the objection so you can get insight into why the client feels the way she or he does. To sell to clients you must know how they think!

Let's look at other counterproductive things salespeople do when they are confronted with an objection. Some just quit; they give up and hang up. Others are more elegant in their surrender; they quit but they do so in an indirect manner. For example, if the client says, "I already have one," they would say something like, "Well, when will you need another one? . . . Fine, I'll call you then in 6 months." They defer to the future without finding out exactly what it is the client has now and how it is working. They should be asking, "Gee, can you tell me what you got? . . . How is it working? . . . How have you found . . . ?" Other salespeople become defensive, even confrontational, contradicting the client with, "No, that's not so" or "No, Mike, the numbers are right." Others agree, using the famous *but* — "I can see that, *but . . . ,*" and after the *but,* they proceed to tell the client how he or she is wrong. Others ignore the objections; for example, the client says, "I'm satisfied with my present . . . ," and the salespeople say, "Well, let me just tell you about . . . " In fact, the better the salesperson's product or organization, the more likely she or he is to do this! Others ask "questions" that are self-serving ways to make *their* point rather than to gather information or find out how the client thinks: "Well, aren't you interested in quality?" (Translated: "You dummy, aren't you aware you have to pay for quality?")

These approaches to objections have two things in common: They *tell* and they are *defensive*. The alternative is to show *empathy* and ask a *question*. The choice is simple. Doing the alternative is not easy and takes discipline.

Questions like "What are you comparing us to?" will help you understand the situation and preserve your deal or price. Good questions give you depth of information that you compare apples and apples and keep both *value* and cost on the table. The empathy statement prefaces key questions helping pave your way by making the client more receptive. If, however, in spite of your prefacing, a client objects to your question and says, "I'm not telling you about other offers!" you can simply say, "I didn't mean to offend you, but packages can look the same yet be significantly different. I can respect your view. . . . " In a sales situation you would back off unless, for example, you are in a negotiation, in which case you might use the broken record tactic and ask your question again. Fortunately, the empathy statement will help reduce the amount of times client's will react negatively. And how the client answers your questions often—even if the answer is negative—will give you insight into what is really going on, whether the objection is a ploy, and how you can counter problems.

Some salespeople do ask the right question, but they don't gain as much ground as they could because they fail to use empathy, to preface, or to cushion the question. These salespeople probably don't use empathy because they are not aware of the value of doing so. They may be following the "old" sales role model in which the salesperson "educated" the client and the salesperson had to be "right." Today salespeople need to discipline themselves to create an interactive dialogue. Regrettably, even today sales training companies teach salespeople to respond to objections with an immediate answer or by asking questions designed to force the client to say yes: "Wouldn't you agree quality is important?"

One sharp sales manager sent me what he called a "believe it or not" list for dealing with objections that he got in a sales course. The objection was the classic, "Your price is too high" objection.

Salespeople were actually advised to respond *immediately* with, "Well, what would you do in my place?" "Like you, we have to make a profit" and "You get what you pay for." On the surface these responses may sound reasonable, but they have very little to do with understanding the client's need, helping to find out why the client feels that way, or showing value to the client. Today this kind of thinking won't get you very far. The focus is on the *salesperson's needs,* and in today's world that is downright backward.

Good role models for selling and common sense seem to be rare. Salespeople need to think about how they want to deal with their markets and clients and what their clients require. A simple principle to keep mind is "Always *help* your clients." *When you help clients you will share in your clients' success.* The objection resolution model is a process that will enable you to help! Today's leading advertisers say, "It's a viewer generation." In sales, it's a client generation.

Position Your Idea.   Once you narrow down the objection with a question, you will be able to address your client's *real* objection. When you know the underlying concern at least you have a shot at fixing it, and your client can help you. Also you won't be swimming upstream, because the client will be involved in the solution or resolution of the objection. You can make the process progress by involving the client. You don't have to persuade in a hard sell way. It isn't likely to work anyway.

You can use relevant features and benefits of your idea or product, your institution, and yourself to satisfy your client's concern. For example, a commercial banker convinced his client (for traditional commercial banking needs) to do a swap with him even though the client had previously done swaps only through his investment bank. The commercial bank used his personal commitment as his value-added benefit. When he narrowed down the objections and realized what was at the heart of them—"Your bank is just not experienced"—the banker said, "*I* personally will make sure . . . " The client did the trade with him because he knew he could count on *his* banker to execute.

Check.   Once you have dealt with the objection, you should not assume your effort satisfied the client. Check to see how your client feels about your response. Although this is important in all selling situations, it is especially important in telephone selling, since you can't see your client's reaction. Simply ask the client how he or she feels about what you have said before you move on to your next point. For example, you could ask, "How does our . . . satisfy your concern about exposure?" or "Bob, if *I* personally assure you it will get done, will you give us a shot?" Checking also will help you avoid thinking you have satisfied a client's concern when in fact you have not. Client may not respond at all—just listen—and salespeople misread this silence from the client as a sign of agreement. Don't learn this the hard way—silence does not necessarily mean agreement.

Checking can help you measure where you are with the client. It can help you save time. By asking, "Did that address your concern?" you can avoid droning on and on when in fact the client already understands and agrees with your point. Although some objections can't be satisfied or offset, checking will help you identify those objections that can be satisfied and allow you to save time; checking can help you tie things down. Many salespeople say things like, "Well, I don't know if that satisfies X" and then just leave the point midair. Salespeople who know how to check would catch themselves and add, "Well, let me ask, does it?"

Working with the Rude or Irate Client

As a part of dealing with objections, let's consider the rude or irate client. The objection resolution model (presence, empathy, questioning, listening, positioning, checking) can help you cope with these clients. The model gives you a process to follow to manage the emotional interference that compounds and often disguises the real problem. Having to cope with difficult clients cannot be avoided, but most clients, fortunately, are reasonable. With those who rant and rave, *you* can remain professional no matter how bad it gets. Consultative selling skills can help create positive situations and avoid inciting negative ones by what *you say and how you say it!* (See Part 2 for more on the six critical skills.)

One top telephone salesperson says he loves obnoxious prospects. He says that because most salespeople would rather talk to a friendly prospect or client, unfriendly ones are not actively pursued. "Since most salespeople don't stick with them, obnoxious people are my *best* source of business. Once I succeed in getting them as clients, they are my *best and my biggest* because there isn't much competition for their business," he boasts. He deals with them successfully by keeping his own ego in tow and by genuinely trying to be *helpful.* Another successful salesperson says "Everyday I expect to talk to someone who will 'blow off steam,' but my job is to turn him around."

Although it's not always easy for most salespeople to "stick" with difficult or abrasive clients, it is important to look at the business potential they offer and to develop the skills and persistence needed to handle them. Even when clients or prospects emphatically say, "Don't call me," you can often keep trying, and many clients will respect your effort. One persistent salesperson called and called his prospect. After pursuing this client for months, he finally got an order from him. Snag: The salesperson was unable to fill it! When the prospect learned this, he went into a rage and told the salesperson *never* to call him again. The salesperson waited 6 months before he picked up the telephone to call, and within two weeks he wrote the largest target ticket of his career with this client. A combination of persistence and patience pays. Another salesperson was denied a face-to-face meeting with a client who said, "Call me for 6 months with ideas (information) and then we'll see." But this salesperson used the value he brought to the client in his phone calls to beat down the time to 6 weeks.

When you meet up with an obnoxious or rude client, don't let that call weigh you down. You need to tell yourself and *believe* that rudeness is a reflection on the client, not you. You can't control every call, but you can control yourself. You'll know if that call "got to you" and is beginning to interfere if you start telling yourself things like, "Well, it's just not a good day to make calls" or if you decide to extend your lunch and are reluctant to get back to calls. Challenge these thoughts by asking yourself why.

Tell yourself and believe that even a wave of "bad" calls may be nothing more than coincidence. Also take the time to critique how you are using your six critical skills (presence, rapport, questioning, listening, positioning, checking). Also ask yourself if you are as prepared as you could be. Take a break, and, under most conditions, set a time to get back to calls. If you really feel stuck, ask your manager to work with you, listen in, and give you feedback. Don't give up.

The objection resolution model can help calm your client and prevent you from becoming hostile yourself. Your empathy statement followed by a question can often help you turn the situation around. Consider how skillfully one executive handled a board member who accused him of being "incompetent." Rather than becoming defensive or aggressive and without agreeing with the client's accusations, the executive asked, "May I ask why you say that?" The board member explained that he was not fit to be president because he lacked technical knowledge (a geological background). The executive then asked, "What do you think is needed?" When the board member shot off a list, he responded to it with conviction and confidence. By the end of the meeting call, the board member was full of apologies. How did the executive turn this around? Empathy and questions. He remained calm and professional. He showed conviction. He was confident. He got to the issue *without* causing the aggressive board member to lose face in front of his peers. By not taking the attack personally, he succeeded in changing the board member's position. Of course not everything works out this well. But regardless of how outrageous the client is, *you* can always remain professional. Remember that the prospect or client's rudeness is a reflection on him or her, *not on you*. The same holds true in aggressive, hostile telephone situations. A salesperson felt attacked when his prospect lashed out. "Yes, I got your letter and I *wasn't* at all impressed by your name-dropping of people here. That holds no weight with me! But that booklet you sent was a clever technique for getting my attention." The salesperson, taken back by the anger in the client's voice, drew on the objection resolution model. He said, "Well, I appreciate the opportunity to speak with you. What was it in the booklet that caught your attention?" By the end of a call that had a rocky start, the client asked for a proposal. What the client needed and what the salesperson offered did not match up, but the phone call opened up a dialogue for future opportunities. Since the model requires practice (although most salespeople *think*/profess they use it), it can help to write it on a card and place it by your phone.

In dealing with difficult clients it is important to keep a positive attitude and recognize that the clients are *not* usually directing their anger at you personally but at their perception of the situation. How you cope with rude or difficult clients is a factor of your own maturity and your ability to manage your own ego, temper, feelings, emotions.

You also need to keep in mind that clients find it easier to be rude over the telephone, since that contact tends to depersonalize the situation. It is similar to what happens to people when they get behind the wheel of a car. In person, for example, on an elevator, the individual might be very polite and graciously step aside so you can pass. But on the highway behind the wheel, the same driver can become a terror, cutting you out. Like the car, the phone can have an anonymous, depersonalizing quality. To cope, use the objection resolution model and develop a genuine respect for your clients. Liking and caring about the client and a willingness and desire to *help* are the cornerstones of working things out.

Don't Take the Client's Anger Personally

Intellectually most telephone salespeople know that it does not make sense to take client rudeness personally, yet they may find it difficult not to personalize the situation. Some people are tempted to respond in kind. One of the key reasons rudeness sparks rudeness is the mental message, "X *should* not behave that way." The word *should* starts a chain reaction which leads to "and I'm not going to put up with it." Dr. Albert Ellis, founder of the Institute for the Advanced Study of Rational Emotive Therapy, advises people to substitute for phrases "he or she should," phrases like, "*It would be nice if he or she didn't act that way*" or

"It is inconvenient that he or she is not . . . " The mental message of "should" or "should not" leads to trouble. According to Dr. Ellis, by eliminating the thought "should," you can change how you feel about the event and therefore your response to it. If you think a client's response is *terrible,* you will respond accordingly.

It is important to remember that no rule says that clients *should not* be rude. By eliminating the idea of "should" and by using the objection resolution model, you can cool down the situation instead of getting into the heat of the fray. Certainly there is no reason to tolerate true abusiveness from clients, but most client rudeness usually falls far short of that. Usually the client is frustrated and is venting that frustration. Your role is to *help.*

> CLIENT: "My statement is wrong again. I am sick and *tired* of *your total incompetence!*"

Don't	Do
SALESPERSON: "Well, don't take it out on me. There is no reason to raise your voice with me. I didn't do it."	SALESPERSON: "I am very sorry to hear that there is a problem with your statement. Let me get some information so that I can help? Can you tell me . . . ?"

This "do" is *not* idealized; it is professional. The job of salespeople is twofold: to sell profitable business and to create a positive image of their organizations. Executive management and line managers should drive both these points across. Most people will agree that manners are on the decline across the board, but it is up to each professional to reverse this trend personally. Like the best-selling book *50 Simple Things You Can Do to Save the Earth,* there are simple things you as an individual can do to provide quality service, even if your corporate culture hasn't embarked on that mission yet. In the "don't" example, the salesperson responded on a personal level. The salesperson took the word *your* as a personal affront, losing sight of the dual objective to sell profitable business and create a positive image for the organization providing the business. Almost as unprofessional as this approach would be showing disinterest—just getting the facts with no empathy. The "do" salesperson is a professional with a clear sense of objectives and the skills to communicate and help the client.

One top salesperson says he *looks* for client complaints. Every time a client complains, he says, "Thank you for telling me. Your candor . . . What . . . We will . . . Is that OK?" Salespeople who are truly client-centered welcome complaints, and after they hear the client out they add, *"Is there anything else?"*

In a recent article in the *New York Times* entitled "Give the Customer What He Wants," Marcus Sieff, former chairman of Britain's largest retailing company, Marks & Spencer, known for its quality and service, tells of an important switch his organization made. Instead of responding by letter to customer complaints, they *telephone* the customer immediately. Marks & Spencer has found that this more personal and immediate approach is "much more efficient and economical, as well as more appreciated by the customer."

Whether you are selling to a corporate client or a retail client, knowing how to turn a negative client relationship around can often result in business. For example, one rep called a prospect. Before she got very far, the client became angry and hostile. She had already been rejected by this very bank for credit. To add insult to injury she said she had been unable to find out why her application for credit had been rejected. The new rep was able to turn the situation around by remaining calm and emphatic. She did not become defensive, adding fuel to the fire. Nor did she join in and attack her own organization with a comment like, "I know, *they* don't know what they are doing." Instead, as a professional, she was empathetic. She said, "Yes, I know how frustrated you must feel. I apologize that you could not get an explanation when you called. This is unusual from my experience, and I'd like to look into it. May I ask, when did this happen . . . ?" By asking questions, the rep got back to business and found a new "in." She learned this rejection occurred more than 6 months before, and after asking a few more questions, she suggested that the client reapply and send her application to the salesperson's attention. Of course, she told the client that she could not guarantee approval. She promised, however, to write on the application, "This client has been turned down. If this happens again, please contact the client and explain why."

It is helpful to know how to disengage from a client who is downright abusive, from one you simply can't help, or from an overly chatty client. Once you identify a situation that needs to be terminated, you could say (*after listening patiently for a while and making suggestions the client rejects*), "Mr. X, I understand (repeat the specific key concerns so the client knows you heard them) and how upset you are." Then respond with what it is you will do. Be patient, use empathy, and if necessary use the *broken record* tactic, repeating yourself. When you can't help the caller there or then, and you have exhausted everything and know it is time to get off the telephone, (1) adopt a slower, more deliberate voice; (2) use client's name and show empathy; (3) repeat the problem; (4) state what you can or will do and what the client can expect; (5) say, "That is what we can do now. Goodbye (name)." If the client begins to talk again, listen. When the client takes a breath, repeat step 5. If the client is truly abusive (for example, using profanities), you should remain consultative but disengage ASAP. If the client is insistent or irrational, you have at least three options: (1) You can tell the client you will put her or him on hold while you refer this to your manager ("Ms. X, I am going to put you on hold while I get my manager . . . "). (2) You can say, "Ms. X, I have taken note of your concern, and I will discuss it with my manager who will get back to you by (time)." Or (3) You can politely disengage by saying, "I am sorry. . . . We will (state what you will do)." In all three cases you should end by saying, "Thank you for contacting us. Goodbye, Mr. X." Wait for a goodbye and hang up. If you have tried to satisfy an objection or complaint with an irate client two times, it may be appropriate to refer to or involve a manager, even if the manager will repeat what you have said, since the same information stated by a manager has more weight.

In summary, the best approach is to let the client express his or her objections and to be empathetic and ask questions. Remember no matter how bad it gets, you can stay in control of yourself. You are a professional. You cannot control what the client initially says, but with the objection resolution model you can often control what happens after that. And you can always control yourself in a sales situation. Again, *empathy* and *questions* are your best tools.

Self-Test Worksheet

Now test yourself. Fill in the blanks as you would approach these objections.

CLIENT: "Your price is too high!"
YOU: (1)_____
    (2)_____
    (3)_____
    (4)_____
CLIENT: "It's just too different for us!"
YOU: (1)_____
    (2)_____
    (3)_____
    (4)_____

Now critique your responses:

1. Did you begin with empathy?   yes__ no__
2. Did you ask a "why" question to get more details?   yes__ no__
3. Did you then tailor your response?   yes__ no__
4. Did you check to see if the client was satisfied?   yes__ no__
5. Do you believe in your product, idea, company — your pricing and value?   yes__ no__

If you missed point 2, please reread this chapter, because this model personifies all that selling for the nineties is about.

5
Framework: Closing/ Action Step

Salespeople are always concerned with closing and rightly so. It is your *job* as the salesperson to *close*. Clients *expect* you to ask for their business or initiate the next step. There are two kinds of closes — big *C* and small *c*. With a *C*lose, you ask for the business, and with a *c*lose, you initiate the next step toward getting it. Both closes most obviously physically occur toward the end of the sale, but closing begins before then. Closing must happen *throughout* the sale and before and after the sale. If you wait to close at the end of the call, you will probably be too late. By making closing a process throughout the sale and getting feedback, you will improve your closing results.

Many salespeople are hesitant to *C*lose (ask for the business) because they are afraid of rejection or they worry that they will close down communications. But the real problem with closing is that many salespeople simply don't know how to do it. Some people have a natural instinct for closing, but most salespeople are no more than average in their closing skills. And this means they get no more than average results. One manager referred to his salespeople as "information junkies," always gathering information but never getting anywhere. The bottom line: They couldn't close. What was wrong? His people were not closing-oriented. They did not have clear call objectives before going in. They did not get client feedback throughout the call. They did not ask preclosing questions. As a result, they were leaving calls not knowing where the clients were and, therefore, where they stood. Other salespeople have different closing problems. They are actually on the road to closing—or in fact have closed—but then "unclose" by bringing up irrelevant or extraneous information, such as what *might* happen in the future. Sometimes these salespeople continue to sell (unsell) and talk themselves out of a sale.

To make closing a process, begin the close early—*before* you initiate the call, when you set your call objective. (See Telephone Call Objective/Purpose in Chap. 14.) Setting a performance objective before the call helps you visualize what it is you want you and/or your client to do at the end of the call, giving you direction and focus.

Keeping this vision in mind you can close *throughout* the sale as you check the client on your ideas *each time* you make a key point or answer a question. Feedback gives you a "moveable base" you can use to measure where you stand and let you know *when* to ask for the business or initiate the next step.

Consultative selling requires at least a 50-50 dialogue with the client. When your client speaks less than 50 percent of the time, your chances of closing diminishes with every percentage point. Checking, asking for client feedback on what you have said, and your questions are the tools you have to create that dialogue. Salespeople who do most of the talking without feedback often find themselves in the unfortunate situation of controlling almost all the call—all but the end when the client says no and they are powerless. They are powerless at this time because they didn't get feedback to understand how the client was responding early on when they might have fixed or adjusted their presentation.

Checking can lower the risk of rejection by helping you close in small steps. The give-and-take process of checking throughout the call helps set up the close. By asking questions like, "How does that sound?" "What do you think?" or, "How would that work?" you can gauge where you are and more importantly where the client is. The process of checking helps involve the client and lessens the extent to which you are out on a limb alone when you close without a clue of where the client is.

The word *closed* has a special meaning. "I closed the deal" means you won the business. But before this happens, you need to do preclosing work not only by identifying and satisfying needs but by asking essential questions that prepare you for closing. You really can't intelligently close unless you have the following kinds of information:

- What is it the client wants to achieve?
- How will the client make this decision?
- How does the decision process work?
- What are the buying criteria?
- What are the client's priorities?
- Who are your competitors?
- What is the client's view of the competitors?
- When will competitors make their presentations?
- Where do you stand/rank among these competitors? How does the client feel about you?
- What concerns, reservations does the client have about you or your organization?
- What are the client's *time frames* for making the decision?
- How does the client's manager feel about the product you are selling? (If the client hasn't discussed it yet with manager, the sales cycle will probably be longer.)
- What is the budget? (Is there one?)

Unless you ask these questions, you won't be in a good position to know when and how to close.

Preclosing questions may seem hard-hitting, but when asked properly they are really basic. One salesperson confided that although he had good calls, he just wasn't successful in closing. He complained that a lot of his clients wasted his time. But when he was asked if he found out early on about his client's time frames, decision-making process, and budget, he said no. But once he was asked that question, his eyes lit up, and it was clear those questions would become a part of his repertoire. Once you get answers to preclosing questions like the ones listed above and use the answers to position your product or ideas (checking all the way), you will be in a good position to close.

When you close, use benefits, confidently and energetically suggest a sales action or next step, and then be quiet. For example, "So that we can . . . (benefit), what amount would you like to roll over so that you can begin to earn interest immediately?" "Everything is set. All I need is your okay (silence)." "We are ready to . . . I think this is the right time (silence)" or "I can get that in the mail to you today so that . . . OK? (silence)" or "If you can get your figures to us . . . When can you send them so we can . . . ?"

Be sure not to miss your client's buying signals whether they are direct or subtle. One new salesperson almost lost a deal because she missed the go-ahead. The client said, "If you can get the information to me by tomorrow morning, we'll do it." Her reply, "If you give us the go-ahead, I can." She completely missed the client's green light—he had, in fact, already closed and had given the go-ahead! Interestingly enough, when she was asked what her objective was, this salesperson said "to get the client to discuss his recommendation with his sons." Her low expectations prevented her from recognizing a yes! Listen for direct and indirect client closes, for example, *"Well, how do we begin?" "What will this cost?" "What is the timing?" "How would it work?"* or other questions about price, start-up, or comments in which clients have mentally put themselves in the situation in which they already bought.

A good example of reading a green light comes from director Andrew Bergman. In a recent interview featured in the *New York Times,* Bergman recalls how when he called Marlon Brando to ask him to consider a "godfather"-type role in his movie *The Freshman,* Brando at first expressed doubt about his ability to act in a comic role. In response Bergman complimented Brando, saying that he had found him hilariously funny as Jor-El in *Superman.* Bergman and Brando spoke for a few minutes more, and Bergman said, "I knew he would do it when (Brando) began to muse about what he would wear."

Once you have asked your closing question, if the client remains silent, don't assume this signals agreement. It does not. Wait. Be patient. If necessary, repeat your question or ask, "Well, what do you think?" Be sure to get agreement, or you may be the only one in the conversation who thinks you have a deal. Also, once you or the client has closed, don't "unclose" by reopening points or introducing irrelevant points. Once you get the go-ahead, be positive, confirm, and hang up. For example, "Done." "We'll do . . . " "Great!" or "We will (summarize what you will do) . . . " End with a thank you.

Of course regardless how clear and confident your close is, there will be many nos and maybes. Clients may say a flat no or may delay things by saying, "I want to think about it." Whenever this happens, your goal should be to find out while you are on the line *why* the client is saying no or what it is the client needs to think about. You can say, "We talked about . . . May I ask what your hesitancy is?" The reason for finding out why the client is resisting is to allow you to address the concern. For example, if a client says, "I don't like the spread," you can ask why. Once you understand what the customer is comparing the spread to and get insight into the client's reasoning, you will be in a better position to position your idea. Ask, "Well, what spread rate are you looking for?" so that you know what the customer will say yes to and turn that into a buy order (okay for you to buy at a particular price).

The best way to close is to approach closing as a process. Begin with an objective, check for feedback throughout the call to gauge where you are, and then ask for the next step (end each contact with a next step to keep things moving along) or for the business!

6
Framework: Follow-Up

Follow-up, the sixth and final element, is an essential part of the telephone sales process. The words on a popular coffee mug, "The sale begins *after* the client says no," are at best partially right, but it reflects the hard-sell, tug-of-war type selling of the past. If you want long-term relationships and a good reputation, the sale really begins after your client says yes—when it is your turn to fulfill your sales promise. And better yet, the relationship begins when you deliver more than you promise. As a sales manager once told me, "Save a little bit when you sell and give them more!" Making good on what you have sold makes for satisfied clients and helps ensure repeat business, referrals, and your all-important good reputation. The real key is to close the sale *and* open the relationship.

Providing excellent follow-up is one sure way to distinguish yourself from all of your competitors. First and foremost, get back to clients when you say you will. Ending each contact with a clear next step and jotting commitments down in your notebook is the way to make this happen. If you don't have the answer or the information the client is waiting for, call the client to give a status report so she or he is not left waiting and wondering.

But problems with follow-up are often related to "sloppy" closing. How can you follow-up *sharply* on a fuzzy close like "I'll get back to you" or "I'll call you next week"? Train yourself to think in a precise manner about follow-up and to *commit* yourself to a next step. Replace a fuzzy, "I'll call you tomorrow," with, "When tomorrow would be a good time to reach you . . . ? Here? Great. . . . I'll call you at 9:30 and we'll have the documentation ready by then too. . . . Thank you." Then write it down on your daily to-do list (your follow-up system) and make that call as promised. Follow-up also means answering all the calls you get immediately, no later than within 24 hours, to maintain a sense of urgency. In a sales or service situation, *never* let a client wait more than one day for a return call. Good follow-up is related to your ability to make and keep commitments. This requires being organized and having good self-management skills, respecting your clients, and living a high-standard work ethic.

Follow-Up When Waiting for a Decision

Ongoing follow-up will also help *you* be the one to win the business when there is a lapse between when you ask for the business and when the client makes a decision. Sometimes it is not possible to get an immediate decision. Although some calls can be split-second decision calls in which the client will say yes or no on the spot, other sales require a longer process. For example, if you are one of several competitors, your client may need to confer with others in the decision-making group or simply to give the decision more thought.

Once you ask for the business, the telephone is an invaluable tool for keeping in touch with your client. Contact can boost you ahead of less attentive competitors. *Stay close* — whether by telephone, letters, or personal visits. One experienced salesperson learned the cost of not doing this. After intense competition he was one of two finalists. In the final face-to-face meeting, it was obvious to him that the two competitors were closely matched, but he felt he had two real advantages over his competition—location and a superior product. His full system was slightly higher in cost, but unbundled it was competitive. In discussing price with his client, the salesperson had matched the competitor's price—with better terms. The prospect, a large computer firm, was to make its decision in the next 2 weeks. For a bizarre reason that even the salesperson can't explain, he "forgot" about this prospect. His busy schedule, other clients, new deals, and so on caused him to blank out about the prospect after his final presentation. Ten days later, when he finally called, he learned the contract had been awarded to his competitor. Why? The "reason" given by the prospect was price. The salesperson learned, too late, that his competitor had lowered his price *and downgraded his maintenance terms*. Surely, the salesperson could have matched the new terms and price easily by making the same type of changes that the competitor made. But the prospect had gotten the deal he wanted from a *responsive* salesperson, so he didn't bother to get back to the salesperson who "disappeared." As a matter of fact, the lack of follow-up further pointed to the advantage of going with the competitor. Lesson: Stay close, keep your hand on the client's pulse, keep your hand on the telephone, and hold the client's hand.

One word of warning: don't suffocate the client or become a pest. One consultant called *too* often during one day to the point of annoying the staff and the decision maker. The consultant was demanding and became annoyed when the client did not return his calls. This, coupled with his appearance at the client's office door at 7:30 a.m. when the client returned from vacation, made the client feel that the consultant was "desperate for business." The client steered clear of him.

When there is a waiting period, follow these guidelines:

- Be sure you know when the decision will be made and what the process will be.
- Get to all decision makers and influencers if possible. Target the ones your competitors have gotten to, especially top people.

- Follow up and find reasons to stay in touch. Say, "I called to touch base and to see if you have any questions" or "I'm calling to thank you for the meeting. . . . " Then summarize one of your strengths. Stay close to the situation. Be creative in finding reasons to stay in touch.

- Find out when your competitors are presenting and create a reason to call your client *after* your competitor's presentation to find out — tactfully — what the client liked, didn't like, and what repositioning you might have to do.

    For example, one software salesperson, during a telephone conversation, learned that the client would be meeting with a competitor that afternoon. As soon as she heard this, she went into gear: "Do they offer . . . ?" "How many installations . . . ?" Without directly criticizing the competitor, she elicited critical feedback from the client and also created questions in the client's mind about the competitor. Most important, she called the client directly following the meeting with the competitor to see how things were progressing and to tactfully get feedback on the meeting. This gave the salesperson a chance to answer any questions raised in the client's mind as a result of the meeting. It also put her back in first place.

- Whenever possible, be the one to make the *last* presentation so that you have the advantage of selling to an informed group and having the last word.

- Make sure your office knows that a decision with X is pending and how to reach or support you if you are not in the office.

Follow-Up after a Face-to-Face Call

Most big-ticket salespeople whose primary client contact is by phone make it a point to meet their clients. And of course salespeople who sell primarily face to face use the phone with their clients. Whether you see your clients once a week, month, or year, the phone can help you keep the benefits of the face to face alive. One top-performing salesperson who sells primarily by phone makes it a point to meet his prospects/customers within 3 months (or sooner) if possible of his first contacting them. He says it is in the face-to-face call that real trust and rapport occur for him, and he attributes this to the physical presence—the handshake, eye contact, and personal meeting. He says he then can use the phone to carry the essence of the face-to-face call forward. Once he meets his clients he knows "how to approach them better" and "how to use their name" and "how far you can go." Many phone salespeople say there is a difference between pre-face-to-face and post-face-to-face phone calls. Certainly after the first face-to-face call, it is essential to call immediately after the call—"Tom, thanks for taking the time to see me"—and to use the call to keep the rapport of the face to face alive and build on it.

Let's look at the skills you will need to make your phone calls seem "face to face."

PART 2

The Six Critical Skills

In each of the elements in the telephone call framework (opening, client needs, positioning, objections, close, and follow-up), you will use the following six critical selling skills over and over *and over*. They are your tools for selling.

- Presence
- Relating
- Questioning
- Listening
- Positioning
- Checking

Your skill level determines your selling strength and flexibility. These skills are used over and over throughout the sales process—as you open, find needs, match up your product or idea with the client's needs, resolve objections, and close, you are continuously using these skills. Your mastery of these skills will help you become a valued consultant to your clients. The skills are interdependent and will help you know more about your clients and sell more to them.

7
Skill: Presence

Presence is hard to define, but it is *real* and it gets *real results*. *Presence* is the level of comfort and confidence that you project. The term *presence* is related to the "stage presence" through which an individual can engage the audience's attention. But presence isn't "showing off." It is said Marlon Brando has an overwhelming presence—the viewers focus on him to the exclusion of others on the big screen. But a voice can have presence, too. Consider the fireside chats of President Franklin D. Roosevelt in which each listener felt that Roosevelt was speaking to him or her personally.

Your voice presence can have an impact on your telephone sales success. Voice presence is created by tone, pace, diction, inflection, level of enthusiasm, confidence, wit, and the ability to think on your feet. For example, just before a 26-year-old associate of an investment banking firm was about to go to Chicago to meet his newly assigned client, he heard the inevitable, "You sound young" from his 60-year-old-plus client. Since the rapport was good, the associate confidently, quickly, and light-heartedly responded, "If you think I sound young, wait until you see what I look like." Both people laughed and an upcoming meeting got off to a good start. More important, the client was prepared to meet his young salesperson.

Your presence helps instill in your clients a feeling they can count on you. Presence shouldn't be mistaken for arrogance. This may work for some (when they are in the cat bird seat, for example and have a *hot* property to sell), but *in the long run* arrogance is *not* good for business and will backfire.

Although sales enthusiasm may come naturally in face-to-face calls, it requires special effort in telephone sales calls. Most salespeople (hopefully) would not appear bored when meeting with a client face to face, but in telephone selling sustaining interest and enthusiasm in your voice can be challenging. It's hard to make dynamic telephone call after dynamic telephone call, especially in a series of calls, if you encounter a few no's in a row. A top-producing stock broker, interviewed in the *New York Times* during the go-go years of the early eighties, even then said that "keeping 'up'" was his greatest problem. One leading firm in the brokerage industry surrounds its trainees with wall-to-wall mirrors so they can be aware of their body energy. Smiling and other expressions of alertness translate to a more positive approach and seem to be related to alert minds and interested voices.

Unless you are conscious of and aware of your presence and how you project, you can slip into a bored monotone, call after call. Since mind and body are normally in harmony, top salespeople often stand up and some even pace as soon as they start selling. The energy permeates their bodies, and they simply can't sit still. Interestingly enough, however, salespeople who automatically stand up when getting into the sale on the telephone don't usually have the urge to jump up during a face-to-face call. They may sit up or inch up in their chairs, but nothing more. The "extra measure" seems to be required only in telephone selling, where voice and words need extra "projection." The point is not to stand up or pace around all day but to use standing and movement to help you get yourself cooking and get and keep the juices going. Whether you stand or sit, remember to smile, even when you are feeling low, to give a boost to your voice or to help your tone be positive especially if you feel your voice is developing an edge.

Presence is created in part by pace. Rushing can say you are nervous; dragging it out indicates a lack of confidence or a lack of preparation or experience. "To everything there is a season," and to every sales call there is a proper timing. You have to listen and check to determine how your timing is, since you don't have cues such as a customer looking at his or her watch. Whatever your pace, stay *calm*.

A nervous voice on the other end of the line is apt to lead clients to feel their time will be wasted and their business is not in good hands. One excellent exercise to use if you feel nervous and know that the nervousness will be heard in your voice is, right before you pick up the telephone, to blow as much air as possible out through your mouth; to get the last bit out, contract your stomach. This exercise will relax your voice.

Presence is also helped by inflection. Flat is boring and dull. If you feel your voice is flat, it may be worth your time to arrange a session or two with a voice coach who can help your sales talk "sing."

The more modulated your voice, usually the more interesting you sound. You can emphasize words with your voice. For example, "I think the time to do it is *now*." You must also develop the ability to hear the words your *client* emphasizes with her or his voice.

Balance your assertiveness with respect for the client. At all costs avoid sounding impatient, annoyed, judgmental, arrogant, or condescending. There is a museum in New York that is closed on Mondays. For years, if you called the museum on a Monday, you would get a recording that was arrogant and condescending in tone. The speaker in a haughty tone informed the caller that the museum is *always* closed on Mondays. His *tone* said, "How could you not know this?" The recording lacked all empathy or customer orientation. Fortunately, management changed the recording. Today the speaker expresses regret that the museum is not open, informs the caller of the hours and days when the museum is open, and graciously invites the caller to visit then.

If your voice doesn't convey a positive attitude, it will work against you in selling. One salesperson got nowhere fast with his prospect when his ego got in the way. The client's secretary had accidentally disconnected the salesperson. Then she kept him on hold for several minutes. This rash young salesperson took the two events as a personal affront. He let his exasperation show through in his voice, and when he finally got his prospect on the line he killed their previous rapport and the conversation quickly ended. Had he recognized that he was becoming hostile, taken a few deep breaths, focused on his objective, and asked himself where it was written that he *shouldn't* get disconnected or put on hold, he would have had better results. He lost his perspective— there is no law that the prospects have to take calls from salespeople or that secretaries are perfect.

Keeping an interested and positive voice when selling over the telephone is even more of a challenge in highly routinized and comparatively unchallenging telephone selling situations. Some selling borders on order taking, when salespeople have to take information only to make a referral to a different division. Salespeople in these rote roles can drift into sounding bored. To avoid this, remember that your key objective *at all times* is to create a positive image for your organization to the client as much as to sell or close profitable business.

An example of a very routinized call would be the one taken from a client on an 800 number calling to have something sent to her. The salesperson, who has to get the client's mailing information for the seventy-fifth time that day, might feel a temptation to treat the call as "just another call." This temptation might be there, but it is not professional. Whether you are taking information or a message for a colleague, remember the following:

Don't say	*Do say*
"Name"	"Thank you for calling." "So that we can get X to you, I need some information. Your name
"Address"	please? Mr. . . . , your address? . . . Thank you. Your X will be to you . . . "
"Your number"	"May I ask for the account number for X account, Mr.____ please?"
	"Thank you."

Small courtesies such as using positive words including please and thank you, avoiding slang or casual conversation, addressing the client by his or her name, mentioning your organization's name, will help increase your telephone presence. These courtesies will help you build rapport and increase your persuasiveness. Above all, they will help you keep a personal, human touch and prevent the technology from taking over. Tape yourself and self-critique. Avoid phrases like "Hi!" "Yea" "I'm gonna . . ." countless "OKs" "Uh huh" or swearing. A very limited use of some casual language may be "normal," but it most certainly should not be the norm for how you communicate with your clients. Of course, presence will be hurt by yawning, smoking, drinking (gulping), chewing gum, eating, opening flip-top cans, etc., when you are on the telephone. Offenses such as these are more than bad manners; they are bad business.

One client tells how he avoided being the victim of a confidence scheme. He detected an occasional slip in grammar which didn't fit the rest of the "salesman's" image and declined the "golden opportunity," he was being offered. The client was not surprised when he saw this "vice president" charged with fraud some time later.

Presence is also helped by word choice. For example, if you say, "I'm *just* calling about X," the word *just* serves to diminish the value of your call. While you should avoid exaggerations, especially in the nineties, when clients are more skeptical and wary of anything slick, you should use positive descriptive words to encourage client action. One institutional salesman successfully convinced a prospect to work with him. When the prospect objected that the salesman's firm was only interested in big accounts like "the Pru," the salesman won him with, *"You* are *my* Pru!"

In conjunction with the other critical skills, presence adds to your sales strength and flexibility and helps you create a flow between your client's needs and your products.

8
Skill: Relating

If you can't relate to your clients, you won't sell to them. This is as much a rule of human nature as it is a rule of selling. Relating is even more of a challenge over the phone, since the phone can depersonalize the situation. Yet it is possible to establish rapport and build relationships over the telephone. For example, in one case a sales manager was assigned by home office to work with an independent branch where both sales and morale were down. For 2 months the only contact the manager had with the branch was by phone. He established rapport, asked a lot of questions, listened, and followed up. He learned what was key and what was wrong. He helped the branch turn the situation around. When he finally visited the branch, he was greeted by the staff, who hung a 6-foot banner across the entrance to the branch to welcome him. When it was time to return home, he boarded the plane with the banner proudly rolled under his arm.

Of course, personal contact helps people relate to one another, and, for this reason, most big-ticket telephone salespeople make it a point to meet their clients fairly soon, often *within a month* or so of starting to work with them. Although many telephone salespeople involved in big-ticket ongoing sales meet their clients—

whether for a formal meeting, a baseball game, or a dinner — an equal number establish excellent relationships with clients they haven't met. The overwhelming view, however, among top performers is that if your contact is primarily by phone, if possible get out and meet the account as quickly as possible to attach a face to a name. If for no other reason, and there are plenty such as trust and rapport, in a telephone call you may get 5 minutes, but face to face you will have at least 20 to 30 minutes.

But when meeting your client face to face *isn't* feasible or practical because of timing, location, numbers of people to reach, product, or (low-ticket) price, the phone can become a tool for developing a trusting and friendly relationship, but the relationship will take more skill and more time. *More* contact through good calls as well as personal meetings can make this possible.

You can develop rapport and establish relationships over the phone if you take the time and you have the know-how. The young customer service representative who asks her prospects if they are college students and learns they "just graduated" instinctively understands rapport when, before she gets on to her call objective says, "Well, congratulations!" Some salespeople instinctively know how to do this, but others do not. They view rapport as something not directly related to business. Yet, as mentioned, chitchat about nonbusiness topics can lead to business rapport.

One salesperson acknowledged that relating was his weakest skill and that he needed help. The simple question, "How was your weekend?" was a breakthrough for him! Although his group teased him by reminding him not to ask that question on a Thursday, they applauded his openness. Although rapport is often associated with the opening, in fact, rapport should flow through the call. With some clients, rapport comes only after you have proven yourself on the business front — being prepared, adding value, following up, and being honest. Although rapport frequently begins at the front end, it isn't limited to the opening. The right spot to ask about the weekend, children, personal interests, may be nearer to or after the close or *after* several calls. And the right time to invite the client to lunch or dinner often is later — not for the first face-to-face call. Often the time to build rapport on a first call can be the end of the call, when you ask a prospect, "So are you planning to get away for this holiday week-end?"

Although you must know when to draw the line, knowing when and how to share information about yourself is also a part of rapport. Sharing personal information can open the door for the client to share too. Successful salespeople do have strong relationships with their clients, but they also know where to draw the line between what is friendship and what is business. A good relationship forms the basis for good business. What is a business relationship but a series of transactions? In most businesses, important transactions don't occur without a relationship. Whether it is primarily a one-time sale or there is the potential for ongoing business, rapport helps form the foundation where a transaction or many transactions can take place. Rapport goes beyond small talk. Rapport is consideration and thoughtfulness; it is trust and value added.

Rapport is big things and little things. One salesperson almost blew it when he was trying to sell a computer system to Coca-Cola Corp. The representatives from Coke were touring the salesperson's headquarters. Thoughtlessly, the hosting company served Pepsi! Although the seniors from Coke made a joke about it, "the wrong choice" helped put that sale on ice. In contrast, rapport was helped when a salesperson wore a 10-year-old-necklace designed by the major jewelry store she was calling on. The first comment from the client was, "I like your taste in jewelry." You can translate these concrete examples into your phone work. *Tell* your client from Coke that you are drinking a Coke.

Rapport is the state of feeling comfortable and confident with someone. Just as most salespeople have a feeling of being comfortable with their customer when rapport exists, there is a feeling of discomfort when rapport is lacking. A lack of rapport usually means there is a feeling of distrust or an absence of credibility. When rapport is lacking, you can use the other five critical skills to help you create rapport. For example, if a client says briskly, "That's not appropriate for us at X. We just don't operate that way," you can use an empathy statement and a question as a way to gain a new footing. You might say, "Yes, John. I know there is a strong culture here. May I ask, though, how you see this as not being appropriate?" Then you might say, "May I ask what you see as more appropriate?" The client will appreciate your interest and the opportunity to present her or his ideas. And your reasonable response may open an opportunity up for you. Whenever you first face a problem in a sales call, draw on your rapport and questioning skills so that you can position, rather than calling on your presenting skills.

Checking (another of the six critical skills, the one in which you ask for client feedback) can also help you establish rapport. First, checking indicates to the client that you respect his or her views and that you want to listen. Second, checking results in your getting client feedback that you can use to recraft how you position your idea. In addition to using the critical skills to build rapport, your *voice* is important in establishing rapport. When you feel that rapport is lacking—when the client or prospect sounds cold—listen very carefully to his or her tone and tempo and try adjusting your tone. You may be so out of sync with the client that you are helping to cause the problem. Some people might call this mirroring technique to adjust your tempo a form of manipulation, but this is not so. It is not manipulation to recognize that you are not in sync and to seek a way to become synchronized or congruent with your client. More often than you might think, a lack of rapport on the telephone stems from two people who are on different speeds and tempos. As the salesperson, it is your job to recognize discord and create resonance.

One U.S. consultant was speaking with a British prospect and sensed the conversation was choppy. The consultant kept interrupting the client because of the delay in transmission. The telephone call was not a good one. After analyzing the first telephone conversation, she knew she had to call her client back, slow down, and wait while the client composed her thoughts. The next week the consultant called back with a single objective, and the call was a success. At the end of the second call the client volunteered, "I'm happy we spoke again. I feel much more comfortable." The content hadn't changed but the tempo and tone of voice had.

Of course, a positive "chemistry" can happen naturally—some people just naturally click. But more often than not, rapport must be earned. Having your client's interest at heart, knowing what you are talking about, having integrity, not wasting your client's time, executing properly, delivering *quality service*, delivering on your sales promise, and following up—these are extremely important. So are the more "personal" touches. Be sensitive not to call, for example, at the start of a religious holiday, or at 8:30 a.m. after a client returns from a one-month trip. Finally, use the phrase "thank you" to build rapport. Always remember to thank the client whether it is for returning your call or for a piece of business. It is amazing today how often the client is the *one* who says "Thank you" and the salesperson who says "You're welcome." The salesperson's role is unmistakingly the thank-you role. Even if the client appropriately expresses appreciation, you should respond by saying something like, "I'm glad I could help. Thank you for calling about . . . "

9
Skill: Questioning

Being able to establish rapport and knowing how to question are the heart of consultative selling. Salespeople who increase their questions increase their sales! Because of the generic product environment of the nineties and the fact that product alone cannot be counted on to be the differentiator, questioning is more important than ever. This is because questions enable you to *position* (tell your story from your client's point of view). But it is easy to fall into the trap of "telling," especially over the telephone. Of course there are times to tell, but how you tell will be determined by what you ask and what you hear. One sales manager said his salespeople think, "I have to write a ticket. I have to write a ticket. I have to write a ticket . . . " and hence they do not listen or question. He said, "If a customer says, 'I'm buying X,' they say, 'Oh, you're buying X; we can offer this.' But what they need to do is stop hawking product and find out what the customer needs."

Clients are usually willing to give information if they think there will be a payback. But salespeople as a group, as surprising as it may seem, resist asking questions. As mentioned, there are two main fears behind this: loss of control and loss of time. Salespeople have countless others as well: fear of seeming unprepared, fear of instigating client objections, and concern about offending their clients. Although there is some justification for each of these reasons, the price of not asking questions is simply too high. Questions are the tool for getting at needs, and questions are the way to get the dialogue going.

First let's analyze some reasons for not asking questions, starting with the primary one—loss of control. Far from losing control, asking questions helps you *gain* control of the sale. Whoever controls the questions usually controls the call. When the client aggressively drives the questions, he or she drives the call. By asking questions, you, as the salesperson, can slow things down and regain control. As for loss of time, this too is a red herring. As previously mentioned, questions can help the salesperson *gain* or *maximize* time by focusing on the client's needs.

As for stirring up objections, it is true that questions can *surface* objections. Questions do not *create* them, however. At least by encouraging a client to express a concern, you have a chance to address it. And although a question might offend the client, most clients, when the question is positioned properly, are not offended and may share information. And, of course, you can soften a sensitive or tough-to-ask question by prefacing it with the reason you are asking—to help the client. This can help you and the client feel more comfortable with the question. Occasionally clients will resent a question even when it has been prefaced with the reason you are asking. When this happens you can say, "I apologize. I didn't mean to offend you. We have seen so much interest in X . . . I wanted *feedback* from you about your reservations." Keep in mind that although a client is not bound to answer your questions, most will if they believe there is something in it for them. Also keep in mind that clients who continue to avoid you or refuse to give you fundamental information could be signaling a lack of sincerity in doing business with you.

Another reason salespeople don't ask the level of questions they should be asking is that they are trained in the traditional product-selling approach. Often in traditional selling questioning is taught as manipulative tactics. For example, salespeople are taught to ask questions that guarantee them a yes. The classic "Well, don't you want your children to be smart?" question of the door-to-door encyclopedia salesperson of the fifties and sixties is a perfect example. Surprisingly, most training programs still teach such questioning skills aimed at getting (forcing) a yes. One new sales book advises salespeople not to ask a question that will reveal their product weakness. For example, the book suggests that if a client says, "I want 'X'" and your product does not offer X, not to pursue why the client needs X. But nothing could be further from how to sell today. Even if you were to ignore the ethical and relationship reasons that would dictate asking why the client needs X, there are sound sales reasons to ask.

First, no product is perfect. You might learn that the reason for wanting X can be offset by a more pressing requirement, or there may be alternative ways to achieve X. Clients often make demands ("I want X"), but upon closer observation the demand may not be what they need. Demands are solutions. As a salesperson your job is to find the need under the demand — the problem that needs to be solved. Second, by knowing why, you can discuss priorities with your client. For example, a client may want X speed of processing but if accuracy is a higher priority, the client may be willing to sacrifice speed for the accuracy she or he needs. And, of course, at the end of the day, to sell a client something that does not do X when he or she *really* needs X is simply no way to do business — not if you plan to stay in business, not if you need repeat business, not if you want referrals, and not if you value your reputation.

There is one additional reason related to the "old" model of selling that many salespeople resist asking questions. They think that adding value means "telling." While it is *true you must add value, give ideas, and offer solutions, it is all a matter of when.* By investing a minute — or ten hours, depending on the situation — to get the lay of the land, you can learn what it is the client wants to achieve and, more important, *why.* Then you can position your products and ideas and differentiate them.

Most salespeople simply do not ask enough questions. For example, an investment professional, in spite of calling a client several times a week with ideas for trades, hadn't seen any business from his client for a while. At the suggestion of his sales manager, he invited the client out for dinner to try to rectify the situation. He said, "I've appreciated all the business we've done in the past. I know we've done some good things together, but I also know we are missing business with you now. I'd like feedback on why, so I can be more on track. John, what do you need from us that you're not getting?" He did not blame or accuse the client. He didn't focus solely on his own needs. He didn't say, "I'm here to see how we can get more business." Because he positioned this tough question well, he learned that his client's strategy was short-term and his ideas simply did not fit. Although he had made telephone contact with the client several times a week, he missed the essence of what the client was trying to do. He simply hadn't been asking questions and lost track of what his client wanted to accomplish.

We can all learn lessons from this example. When the client said no, the salesperson should have asked *why*. It seems so simple. Yet the word *why* is the most underutilized "power" word in selling, especially over the telephone where you don't have the benefit of visual cues. When clients tell you what they want, they are in a sense telling you the solution. Unless you are strictly an order taker, you should also find out the *why* behind what the client wants. A good example is how every day salespeople too quickly take a client's request for "specs" and run with them without finding out what the client really needs. Unfortunately, the client's solution may not be the best one for the client or the sales organization. A simple question such as *why* can get to what the client *needs* are behind the demand (Like the Rolling Stones' song, "You can't always get what you want . . . but, if you try sometimes, you get what you need.").

A case in point is a client who says, "I need an answer by to-morrow" when, in fact, he or she needs only *one* specific piece of information. By asking, "We'd like to get that for you. May I ask why do you need that so quickly?" you probably would learn a lot and could get needed information to the client without compromising quality or throwing your production into a turmoil.

One salesperson was in a difficult situation. For more than a year he had given free research, market information, and so on to a prospect who never did a trade with him. Finally this salesperson decided to take a risk and pop the question. He tactfully said, "X, as you know, we have been providing . . . over the past . . . How have you found getting this information?" Getting a positive response from the client, he continued, "Great. I know we haven't done any business to date. . . . I'd like very much to continue . . . I'd like feedback to see where I can be more on track so we can do some business together. What can I do to make this happen?" Apparently, the client valued the research and got the hint. He started with some small trades, which soon increased.

Questions will help keep you on at least a parallel track and eventually get you on the same track as your client. Most salespeople simply tell the client why he or she should do X instead of probing. They go counterflow, and that is counterproductive. For example, your client says, "I don't want to meet with him" (referring to a third party critical to the deal). A good salesperson would try to find out why rather than immediately trying to force a meeting.

Questions will also help you *qualify* clients. A major computer company launched a telephone selling campaign to reach new names. The objective was to get the clients to accept a mailing which would be followed up by telephone. The salespeople succeeded in achieving this objective, but the final results were poor. Why? The reps, who normally sold face to face, failed to qualify the prospects to whom they sent their expensive packets and brochures, which went to people in firms that had neither the budget nor plans to change systems. Had the reps simply asked, "May I ask what your time frames are?" or "To make sure we fit with your plans, may I ask what are your plans, may I ask what your budget is?" time and money could have been saved.

Good qualifying questions do more than qualify. They open avenues for discussion and create inroads to finding out what is going on. For example, one client responded to the budget question by saying, "Well, we really don't have a specific budget in mind, but we've seen prices all over the place—from $15,000 to $45,000." The sales rep responded, "I understand. There are so many variables. How far are you in looking at systems? What is more important to you . . . ?" The sales rep was able to uncover information about what competitors the client had been speaking to and what he liked and didn't like. This information gave him an edge that helped him win the business.

Questions, as stated earlier, can help establish rapport. One consultant warmed up what started out as an unfriendly telephone call. When his prospect mentioned a conference he was attending, the salesperson picked up on this and asked more about it. The prospect was quite enthusiastic about the subject. In the process of opening up on the topic, he opened up to the salesperson.

But most important, questions help you identify client needs and strategy. When one investment manager called his client, the executive placed $200 million with him in an overnight instrument, a big drop from the $400 million he had traditionally placed each day for the past 2 years. This sharp salesperson inquired about the change: "Since we've done . . . May I ask why the change?" At first the client explained they were just reducing amounts they invested with banks. But with a second question and rapport, the salesman got a jump start on all his competitors when he learned about a top-level strategy meeting to be held in two weeks, the new criteria for investments, and an opportunity to be the one to help his client shape his presentation to the board.

Whether it takes several questions or one, the key is to ask questions and listen. Many salespeople would be surprised to hear an audio tape of one of their calls to learn how few questions they ask and how narrow their range of questions is. There really is no magic to asking questions. It starts with truly respecting that your clients know more about their situation and business than you do and then listening with an ear to find out more. Then it takes skill so you can question without grilling your clients. Let's look at the range of questions you will need to ask and then the questioning skills you should employ to ask them.

Range of Questions

Decision-Making Questions

- Who are the key contacts on the account—decision makers and influencers?

    "How does your decision-making process work?" "Who will be involved?" "How long do you need to reach a decision?"

Relationship Questions

- "How are we doing?" (How the client sees the relationship with you, performance, and his or her relationship with competitors.)

- "Am I doing the right thing?" "What do you want me to do?" (Action steps.)

  (How you as an individual salesperson are meeting the client's needs.)

- "How satisfied have you been with our service except for this? How do you feel we handled . . . ?"

- "Is our billing detailed and timely enough for you?" (Logistics of the account.)

- "When is a good time to call?" "When shall I call back?"

- "May I ask who you do business with?" "Who is the best? What do you like about them? Who else do you work with?"

- "Who else have you spoken to? Have you gotten proposals? What do you think . . . ?"

Operation Questions

- "How do you do it?" (How does the client's production or organization work?)

- "How many or how often . . . ? What is their . . . ?"

- "What budget have you set?" (Does this customer qualify?)

Problem Questions

- "What is going on? What would your ideal situation be?" "What gaps do you see? (Don't ask this question too early—the right to have it answered must be earned.)

Strategy Questions

- "What is your strategy/thinking in . . . ?"

- "May I ask why you want to go from X to Y?" (For example, manual to computer—find out why the customer wants to change.)

- "How will . . . affect autonomy of . . . " (Changing roles in client organization.)

- "Longer range, how are you . . . ?" (Checking the 5-year plan.)

Interpersonal Questions

- "Where do you live?" "Where do you go on vacation?" (What are the client's interests, family, situation?)

Need Questions

- "What are you looking to achieve?" "How is that working?"

- "To what extent have you bought . . . ?" (Likes/dislikes—what does the client buy/not buy?)

Questions are the tools to help you help your clients. They get beneath the surface of demands, and they expose needs. When the client says, "I don't like it," it is tempting to try to persuade him or her to like it, but more often than not that is a futile effort—a-tit-for-tat—where even if you get the last word the client normally wins. You will get further with a question to help you find out what's behind the client's thinking: "So Sue, may I ask what it is you don't like?" Once you ask a question, take full advantage of it—be silent, listen, use the information.

The following questioning skills can be invaluable to you as you expand your range and number of questions.

Preface. To make both you and your client more comfortable with your questions and to help you ask *tough* questions, soften the question with an introductory explanation of why you are asking. As you preface, show the client the reasons or benefits to the client in answering the question.

Prefacing shows sensitivity and makes the client feel more comfortable. This is particularly helpful for those tough-to-ask questions such as, "What return are you getting?" "What is your budget?" "Who else are you looking at?" "What are the numbers?" A phrase such as, *"So I can make sure I am on track with your budget,* may I ask what amount you . . . ?" can make everybody more comfortable and make clients willing to talk. Another example would be to lead into your question with, *"So that we can focus on the investments best suited to you,* may I ask how much you want to invest?" or *"So that I can see if there is a way we can reduce your exposure,* may I ask what . . . ?" or *"For your protection and security,* may I ask . . . ?" "To see if we can help, what has been your performance in . . . ?" "I know the press has been . . . , and these are challenging times. . . . What has been the effect of the lower rating on your . . . ?" Prefacing questions like this will raise the comfort level of you and your client. One computer salesperson semijokingly said the way he prefaced a price-qualifying question was to say, "Since my boss is going to ask me, can you tell me what kind of budget you have?" Prefacing lets you "give" so you can get.

Trade. Trading is a special type of prefacing in which you offer information in exchange for information. For example, you may say, "We are seeing . . . in this soft market. . . . What are you seeing here?" This give and take can take the "sting" out of a question and can help you to ask a question. Trading also helps render the client more willing to answer your question. Trading shows sensitivity.

Tag Why. Almost no questioning skill is more important than this. A tag why is a process of asking why after a client tells you something to find out more. Ask *why* to *penetrate the surface of a comment* that your client makes. If a client says, "We have . . . Eurobond. . . . " Before presenting your idea you can ask, "Why is that?" or "May I ask why you are interested in . . . ?" One superb sales manager teaches the tag why technique to all his new people. He promises them a big pay off if they get into the habit of asking why. *Tag whys help you get to what the client will or will not buy.* They help you penetrate objections and enable you to get to the heart of the issue and avoid tangents.

Ask Flow Questions. You can make Tom Peter's phrase "close to the client" a reality for how you communicate with your clients. Flow questions require good listening skills because they require that you pick up on "wide" words. These words are ambiguous or vague words the client uses that hold the key to important information. It is in the area of flow questions that the "science" of selling becomes an "art" because it takes an ear. Such words have room for many meanings, and it is your job to get down to the essence. Like a laser, flow questions get inside and behind wide words. When a client says, "We are *worried* about entering that market," you need to recognize that the word *worry* is not a lean, clear word. It is begging for clarification. Once you are attuned to this, these words jump out at you. But most salespeople try to satisfy the "worry" without really understanding what it is all about. Once you ask a flow question, you can enter the word and enter the client's head. You have to be intuned with yourself and the client to go into "flow." It is where great selling and great consulting intersect. "What kind of things are causing you *concern?*" The purpose of asking such a question is to go deeper into the issue, not around or over it. In this way, you can create a flow which gets you and your client in the same groove— headed to a *C*lose, if you can meet the need. You can use such flow questions to understand your client's thinking. The opposite of flow is to contradict, argue, or disagree. For whatever reason, these kinds of responses surface quickly, but with awareness and practice you can get a feel about when to step back and learn more *before* telling your perspective. For example, when your client says, "Frankly, I like X (your competitor)," you can train yourself to ask why, "What is it you like?" Or if a client says, "It's too *rich* for us," ask, "Why is that?" When a client says, "I have *hesitations,*" ask, "What are the hesitations?" *X, rich, hesitations* are all wide words that need to be pared down. There are layers and layers of possible meanings in them. It may seem obvious that these words need to be probed, perhaps too obvious to mention, but most salespeople do not try to get to the real concern before responding. Flow questions, once you develop a sense for when to use them, will be the most natural things in the world. Developing the art of asking a flow question takes practice and discipline. The art takes listening with a third ear—a "need" ear. The payoff for developing this technique is tremendous!

Flip the Question. Even if a client's words are not wide, you may want to ask a flow question to get inside his or her head. One 77-year-old landowner said to a shopping center developer, "Will shops be open on Sundays?" The salesperson, judging by the age of the landowner, assumed he would be against shopping on Sundays. Fortunately for the salesperson though, he asked a question—"Before I respond, I'd appreciate knowing what are your feelings on this, since you know this area." The landowner responded that Sunday shopping was absolutely necessary for the project to work. Some clients, of course, may be wary of the salesperson who answers a question with a question. They may say, "I want to hear *your* ideas." But often they are asking the question *because* they have a view that they want to express. Even if the client had been opposed to Sunday shopping, the salesperson, although he couldn't hide the fact that Sunday shopping was a part of the plan, could have more sensitively positioned his rationale.

Another time to flip the question back is when clients ask questions that ask for your view of something, especially if they consider themselves an expert on the subject. For instance, a client may say, "What do you think the market will do?" Again, often the client has a view of the market. Use your judgment if you think you should present your view first to make sure you don't appear to be trying to skirt the issue. But keep your response *short* and then ask, "Well, what do you think?" One consultant says he learned about this trap the hard way and almost always when a client says, "What do you think of X?"—especially if it is a senior person—he says, "It sounds like you have some thoughts on that. May I ask your view?" Only rarely does he meet with the challenge of, "I asked you *first!*" When that happens he presents an idea or two and then checks with, "How does that seem to you?" or "What do you think?" The point is not to be a chameleon but to have the information you need to position your approach.

Control Questions. Questions can help you maintain control— either to adhere to your agenda or to purposefully deviate from it. Whether you stick to your agenda or change it should be a matter of conscious choice. By having an agenda for each call, you will have a clear sense of what you want to accomplish. You want to remain flexible, but having a set agenda gives you a home base. You can use questions to adjust your agenda in order to align it more closely with client's agendas. You might say, "I wanted to cover A, B, C. How does that meet your expectations for the meeting? Anything else?" Also, if you see that the meeting is going off track and you feel it is time to get back on track, you can use questions to redirect the conversation.

There will be times when your agenda is off track. This could be the result of not doing your homework adequately or from a misunderstanding. Sometimes the client's needs may change, and the client may want to address a pressing need not on your agenda. When the client has a different agenda in mind, you can use questions to find out what and why and then reset your strategy.

If a client goes off on a topic that really is irrelevant to your purpose for calling and is not likely to lead to business, you can use a question tactfully to get back on track. This will help you prevent clients from wasting your time, for example, going on and on (complaining) about factors neither of you can do anything about. A question will let you test how willing the client is to get into a productive discussion. Questions can help you maintain credibility when an issue comes up that is out of your depth. By saying that you want to look into the issue further or that you want to discuss it with a specialist in your organization and then asking questions to understand what the client needs to know, you can show you are serious about getting an answer—the right answer.

You can also use questions to help regain control from an aggressive client who is firing questions at you. For example, a client may be rattling a series of questions at a salesperson who is answering question after question. A way to break the "attack" and regain control is to break the cycle of customer questions by asking a question.

Ask One Question at a Time. Many salespeople ask two or three questions strung together. If you attach two or more questions together, some of your questions will go unanswered. Or your clients will select the questions they want to answer and ignore the rest. Sometimes it can be a strategy to ask two questions together—as a way to hedge your bet if you are not sure which direction to take—but this should be done consciously.

Avoid Answering Your Own Questions. Many salespeople ask good questions but then answer the questions themselves. When you ask a question, be quiet. Don't give multiple-choice answers and don't pontificate. People often do these things because they feel uneasy about asking the question or because they are using questions rhetorically. But prefacing the question with a client-sensitive reason for asking can add to your comfort.

Don't Jump In and Ask a Question for the Client. If your client says that he or she has a question, don't second-guess him or her by suggesting what the question is. Some salespeople do this out of nervousness, a desire to be "on top of things," or *defensively* because they expect a question that will point to their weakness. Unless you can truly read minds, and even then, avoid doing this. One sales rep will probably not make this mistake again. After he presented information on his company, talking about the types of clients and industries they had worked with, his customer said, "Well that sounds great. But I have one question." The sales rep volunteered the question. He guessed it was the one point he had been worried about—his lack of experience in that client's industry. He ventured, "What is our experience in your industry?" The client seemed surprised and then said, "Oh, ah, yes, that too. Well then, that makes two questions." Of course, the point of industry experience would have been covered later; the salesperson set himself in the worst light for addressing it.

Maintain Silence. Be patient. Give your client an opportunity to answer your questions. One salesperson said he *now* waits 5 or so seconds as a matter of course. This conscious effort on his part has made it clear to him that he was jumping in too soon while some of his clients were still formulating their thoughts.

Give Feedback/Don't Be a Battering Ram. Listen to what clients say, and before you ask your next question, make a comment that refers to what the client said. Feedback serves as positive reinforcement and helps you avoid sounding like a prosecuting attorney with a battery of questions. It encourages the clients to keep providing additional information. For example, if the client says, "I was impressed with the report," you could give feedback on that comment such as, *"That's great to hear. Your staff was very helpful in providing . . . so we could do such a thorough report* (give credit back to the client). . . . Anything in particular . . . As you know, there are three phases in the report. Which shall we . . . ?" If, in response to your question, your client explains all the departments that report to him, *before* asking your next question you might say, "Gee, that's quite a big responsibility . . . how do you handle it all?" Especially over the telephone, if you fire away question after question, your client is likely to tire of the one-way exchange. As you listen to your client, remember he can't see you. Verbalize your reactions — all the physical signs that you are listening such as head nodding, smiles, your taking notes, etc. — "Okay, I got that (if you are taking information)" or "Yes," "Uh huh," "That's great," or "That's a riot!"

Avoid Hostile, One-Up, and Tangent Questions. In a selling situation don't use questions that put clients on the spot or show clients that they are wrong and how smart you are. Let's consider the possible responses to a client who says, "But your fee is just too high." Many salespeople become defensive explaining why the price isn't too high. Others ask a question but they ask the wrong one. The "wrong" question is one that dodges the issue by asking the question we critiqued earlier, "Don't you want to save money?" or, more subtly, "Well, how important is quality to you?" What the salesperson is trying to do with the first question is get a yes hoping it will lead to more yeses. In the second question, the salesperson wants to show the client that price is related to value and vice-versa. The problem is that these questions are not based in client needs. The key is to penetrate the objection with a why to find out what makes the client say the price is too high and what the client is comparing you to: "What are you comparing it to in thinking the price is high?" Only when the salesperson has the answer to this can he or she compare value in a meaningful and measurable way. Without this information, the question can seem so presumptuous and offensive. It could imply, "Quality isn't important to you, but it *should* be" and lead to a confrontation. The question is really no better than the primitive one we critiqued earlier, "Don't you want to save money?"

Avoid Going from Demand to Demand. If a client says, "I can't accept $4000 a month!", don't ask, "Well, what figure did you have in mind?" That question takes you from one demand to another demand. You may get to that later to get a parameter, but certainly not early on. Instead ask a *why* question so that you can get to the heart of the objection – get from the *demand to need*. By asking, "What is that?" . . . "What is your current cash flow?" you can get at the need. Demands appear inflexible and unnegotiable, but with needs there is more flexibility and room to satisfy them. In answering, the client in the difficult situation would recognize that $4000 was only $100 a week more than what he was presently paying.

Check. Since you can't see body language over the telephone, you will have to find ways to get a reading of the client's reactions. One excellent way to do this is to check by asking a question aimed at getting feedback after you give information. For example, ask, "How does that sound?" "How would that work?" "We could approach it X or Z. Which seems better at first glance?" "When would you need it?"

Questioning is not a substitute for homework or a shortcut for preparation. But it is the best way you have to gain in-depth information and make inroads to the client. Good questions are the best way to create a flow with your clients. Of course to achieve this you need both planned and spontaneous questions. For example, in planning a call based on your homework you might decide to ask, "In your annual report, there is mention of your trade with the . . . How does that . . . ?" Once you are on the call and the client mentions X, you might ask, "You mentioned you are presently using X. . . . How is that going?"

The questions you ask are important. Unless you are an exceptionally skilled questioner and listener, you should take time to prepare the questions you will ask before the call. The hardest questions to construct are the ones that get beyond what the client is currently doing to what the client needs. Your planned questions normally should not make up more than 75 percent of the questions you will ask and the ideal percentage is 50. Planned questions will open up opportunities for you to ask the spontaneous questions that will give you depth of information. Being able to move from planned to spontaneous questions takes a trained ear that listens carefully and the ability to ask questions that get to the why and how. Your spontaneous questions are like deep sea diving but you need your planned questions to get you in the water. Using both planned and spontaneous questions, your goal should be to ask questions so that *each time you speak with a client you learn more* and know more about your clients than your competitors do. The greater your knowledge of your client, the stronger the relationship you will have.

Of course, questioning is a two-way street. Once you ask a question, your client expects to get something back. At the very least they expect relevant ideas, recommendations, or information—if not immediately, in subsequent contacts. In situations in which clients don't get a payback, the stream of information to you will dry up.

Responding to Client Questions

Because of the spontaneous aspect of questions from clients, questions from them give you an excellent opportunity to build your credibility. No one is expected to know everything. But being as prepared as possible and being able to think on your feet will carry enormous weight with clients. Of course there will always be times when you don't have an answer or are not prepared to answer a question that a client asks. For example, your client may ask about a news article he or she saw in the newspaper that you missed, an advertisement you are not familiar with, technical information appropriately directed to a specialist, or something from left field. Since your credibility is at stake, when *you don't know the answer to the question, acknowledge that you don't.* Don't guess and risk giving wrong information and losing your credibility. Clients need to count on what you tell them. As the old adage goes, "The clock that strikes the thirteenth chime, not only discredits itself but all the chimes before it." When you don't have an answer, take the time to make sure you understand the question. For example, you may say, "We have specialists that . . . , but let me ask what motivates the questions so we can address it properly?" or "Is an acquisition of a low-tech company something you are considering at this point?" Then once you do understand what the client wants to know, jot it down, research it, and follow up as promised.

A word about going on a wild-goose-chase. Some questions from clients call for a tremendous amount of research. Your clarifying questions will not only help you understand what the client wants to know but may also save you from investing a considerable amount of time only to learn the client didn't really care about the point. So when you get a question, be sure to find out what the question is, what motivated it, and when the client needs an answer. Then ask, "I will get back to you on . . . Will that be okay?" If it is a simple question, "May I put you on hold so I can get that information for you?" is appropriate.

Sometimes you only get one shot, so it is important to be as prepared as possible. The key is to anticipate your client's questions. Many salespeople feel uncomfortable about being caught short. If you are unsure of your answer, it can help to draw some preliminary conclusions based on the question if you can and then carry the thought forward by suggesting the avenue it might lead to. For example, you could say, "I didn't give that as much thought as I should have but considering X and Y (what client brought up) then it could affect Z. Let me look into it. . . . " But don't give inaccurate information, and of course get back to the client as promised. That in and of itself can be a differentiator, since follow-up is an area where many of your colleagues will fall short. One salesperson in a crucial face-to-face sales call in New York City had his specialist in Switzerland literally on call by the phone to answer any technical questions that would come up in the meeting. A question did come up, it was handled, and he got the business.

Even when you know the answer to a question—or think you do—show the client you value the question and take a moment to think before you answer. Don't be glib. Never belittle the question with a thoughtless comment like, "*No,* that is not right because . . . " You will be more effective by saying, "*Yes,* John (or Mr. Scott), that is an important consideration, and, therefore, we have . . . "

Also, don't disqualify yourself by being a purist as you answer a client's question. Find out how married the client is to the idea and then position accordingly. For example, if a client asks about a technology or approach you do not advocate, comment generally and then ask him or her how he or she feels about it. Listen carefully not only to what the client says but to how he or she says it, his or her choice of words, and which words he or she underscores. Unless there is an ethical or legal consideration involved, be flexible in how you deal with your product. Certainly, if the client is taking a course of action you feel won't work, explain your reason and give your council but at the end of the day remember it is the client's decision. When a sales manager was asked why his people needed X, he said, "Well, Tom says so and *I* agree," really stressing the "*I.*" The vendor knew to back off from trying to dissuade the sales manager from doing X. It was not that important and persuing it would be a no-win situation for him.

When a client asks a question that in your view is out of sequence, don't table it for later until you consider all the ramifications. Sometimes you can and should table questions until later, but in some situations that is a no-no! For example, if you are speaking with a *senior* person—such as the president of the company or the manager in a group situation—try to accommodate her or his questions on the spot, even if you give an overview answer with a promise of follow-up a bit later. Also, any time other clients are also present, for example for a conference telephone call, be sensitive to how you table something. If you offend anyone, no matter how junior, you are likely to pay for it sooner or later. Although it is appropriate at times to table things, give the client who asked the question your reason for holding the question to make him or her look good before his or her peers or seniors. For example, you could say, "That's a key point. Since it is such an important point (or since it fits in with X), would you mind if I covered it at . . . ?" Be sure to cover it later, and, when you do, refer to the person who raised the point.

Since time is compressed in telephone selling, and since you can't visibly gauge the client's response, don't be long-winded when you answer a question. Respond and check. You can *check* by asking a simple question such as, "How does that answer your question?" or "What do you think of that?" or "How does that sound?"

Questions from the client point you in the right direction and help you hone in on what is on the client's mind. Most clients literally will tell you how to sell to them if you listen. Clients will reveal needs, problems, plans, approaches, and reactions to your ideas with their questions. In the negotiation for the world-renowned Plaza Hotel in New York portrayed in the *New York Times Magazine*, one of the negotiators said that he learned about his opponents' strategy by the questions they asked. Questions from clients can give you insight into how the client feels about you. Are the client's questions aggressive? Are they aimed at your weak spot. Are they supportive?

If you don't let clients talk, you may never get to know what their concerns are, and you will probably miss getting their business. Questions are the best way to get them to talk; then you must listen well and leverage what you learn.

10
Skill:
Listening

Listening/Verbal Cues/Verbalizing Body Language

Body language experts agree that most of the information that is communicated person-to-person comes from nonverbal signals. This has obvious implications for telephone selling where salespeople do not have the benefit of nonverbal signals. Even without facial expressions and body language, salespeople can pick up such nonverbal clues as tone of voice, emphasis, pace, and diction if they are observant.

Being a good listener is one of the critical skills in selling, whether the selling is face to face or over the telephone, but listening is even more important in telephone selling. To gain as much as possible from the telephone conversation, listen not only to what clients say, but to *how* they say it or do *not* say it. Your client's tone of voice (interested or disinterested), pace (relaxed or anxious), voice (positive or annoyed), demeanor (formal or relaxed and more friendly), or silence or absence of a response (thinking, negotiating) all can often give you as much information about the client as words and gestures. For instance, when a client's voice trails off at the end of a sentence or softens on key words, he or she may be giving you a clue about a lack of commitment. Lucky that a publisher was able to hear this. She said she knew that the president of the large company seeking to acquire her small publishing company was *not* in a position to do the deal when the president's otherwise confident and strong voice softened and lowered, becoming tentative on the word "it" when at the very end of the telephone conversation he said, "We'll do it." The publisher hung up realizing that the likelihood of that deal going through was very small, and indeed in one week the president was fired and the deal he was negotiating was off.

Also the kinds of questions the client asks can give you insight. For example, technical detail questions from an engineer, questions about safety from older clients, or questions about risk versus questions about reward can be strong indications of what the client will or will not do.

Once you pick up a signal through listening you can *check* or test the client. A salesperson, quoted in the *New York Times Magazine,* showed that he was a great listener when he told how he knows when a prospect isn't in the deal: "When I told him the price and I heard him *gulp,* I knew he was out. I was on to my next call."

Because your clients can't see you, you need to be aware of the nonverbal cues you transmit. Your tone of voice and your level of animation and interest will be factors in how your clients read you. Although you don't want to become a caricature of yourself, and, of course, you want to be natural, to a certain extent you need to exaggerate your delivery when you are on the telephone. It is important to know when to communicate excitement and emotion, and it is also important to know how not to show signs of fear or impatience when you should be playing poker. In *Bonfire of the Vanities,* by Tom Wolfe, the main character of the novel heard desperation in his own voice and feared that his clients would hear it too! Be aware that your attitude—sarcasm, boredom, unhappiness, or elation—can come through in your voice.

Since clients can't see your reactions, you need to *verbalize positive feelings*. For example, a client can't *see* your smile, so you need to make sure your client can "hear" it with a laugh or comments like "OK," "That's great," "Oh, that's funny."

Other ways to show you are listening are to ask relevant questions, make relevant comments, and acknowledge comments with responses like "Yes," "Unhuh," "Wow." More importantly, *incorporate* your client's words into your responses. It is very effective and persuasive to be able to hear and incorporate the client's key phrases. For example, repeat a pet phrase with a comment such as "Yes, I can understand why you'd want the *historical spread.... How...?*" Picking up and incorporating neon words—words that light up in the client's voice—will let your client know you are tuned in. Taking notes in a face-to-face situation is clearly a way to show you are listening and have regard and concern for the client. Although your client can't see this attentiveness while you are on the telephone, you can say, "I've made note of that," to show your caring and intention to follow up.

When someone (at least in the U.S. culture) looks at you as you speak, it is a good indication that the person is listening to you. Conversely, when someone stops looking at you, you can be fairly sure he or she has stopped listening. When people glance down as you talk, they are signaling consciously or unconsciously that it is their turn to talk. Since you don't have the benefit of such signals over the telephone, keep your presentations short, and check as you go—"What do you think?" Also, even though your clients can't see you, they can sense if you are not listening. So when you speak to the client, stay focused. Don't try to go through your mail when you should be concentrating on what your client is saying!

Few people are naturally good listeners. Most people who are good listeners do not attribute this to being born with good listening skills. Most say it is the result of hard work. Some tips for developing your telephone listening skills are:

- Do *not* interrupt. Be conscious of this. Let yourself *be* interrupted; stop talking and listen.

- Make an effort to focus on what the client is saying. You are "on duty," so stay tuned in. Don't mentally abandon your post. Take notes as you listen and underline words your clients underscore with their voices so you can incorporate them in what you say.

- Listen for *pivotal* words, wide words, key ideas, words that are inflected, and concerns and *jot them down*. These can be neon words that light up the client's voice or wide or ambiguous words you will need to clear up. One frustrated client said that he used the word *synergy* four times over a period of about 8 minutes as he explained what he was looking for in the promotion he wanted to run. Not *once* did his salesperson pick up the word and incorporate it into his discussion of how his product mix would accomplish the client's objectives! Little wonder the client said he didn't feel he and the salesperson were in sync. You can use a worksheet like the telephone contact sheet (Fig. 10-1) to take notes *and* keep a record of your conversations.

- Listen for tone and pace and match both to become congruent with the clients, not to mimic them. For example, if the client is speaking softly and slowly, you are bound to be out of sync if you are loud and fast. Slow it up and soften it a bit to create a congruency. Pick up the client's approach and language. For example, when the client is upbeat and highly articulate, be upbeat, articulate; when the client is serious and straightforward, be serious, straightforward. If you are calling an older client who speaks slowly, slow down. Always be professional. Avoid being down.

- Be careful in how and when you use jargon. Jargon is good shorthand only *if* everybody understands it. Often in a face-to-face call you can read confusion or a question from the client's expression, but over the telephone this is not possible. So limit your use of jargon unless you are absolutely certain the client is familiar with it. When you do use a term that your client may or may not know, briefly define it, almost parenthetically. And as you cover each key point, remember to check if the client has any questions.

TELEPHONE CONTACT SHEET

Customer/Prospect: _____   Contact: _____
Phone: _____   FAX: _____
Salesperson: _____   Call Initiated by: _____

Purpose of Telephone Contact:

Agenda Topics: Reactions/Responses:

Information for File:

Next Step: Customer Time Frames:

Who:

When:

Internal cc: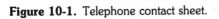

Figure 10-1. Telephone contact sheet.

Note Taking

Taking notes can be the telephone equivalent of eye contact. Not only will taking notes help you focus, it will help you position by incorporating your client's words and ideas. For example, one fabric salesperson, listening intently as his client discussed a lower price offered by a competitor, jotted down the words "on the surface." After this $1 million dollar client spoke for about 5 minutes, the salesperson said, "You mentioned these fabrics are *similar on the surface*. You know we have given you quality . . . your store sold out our garments . . . reorder . . . Can we compare . . . ?" He then proceeded to get *below* the surface and was able to discuss price and value to preserve his price.

Notes also provide you with a *record* for follow-up and documentation. As you improve your ability to take notes, you can increase your client knowledge. Just as salespeople need to improve their listening skills, many need to improve their note-taking skills. It was no accident that in school the students who took the best notes often got the best grades.

When the head of the M&A group of a leading investment bank was asked what he attributed his enormous success to, he spun his chair around, opened a file drawer, took out a sheet of paper and said, "Listening." He added, "Look at this paper. I just got off the telephone with a new client. I always get five or six pieces of information, *not just numbers,* that I can use." He maximizes every telephone call, whether it is to start a relationship or close. He said, "I use the telephone to build relationships and do business. Last week I called a client who is the son of a minister to wish him and his family a Happy Thanksgiving. Today I called him to close a deal."

Note taking, along with letter writing, may be a dying art. Most people just don't take advantage of taking notes when they are on the telephone or face to face for that matter. Not taking notes is related to not being a good listener and not asking enough questions. There is almost a stigma against taking notes. Some salespeople actually think they should not take notes in face-to-face meetings. Of course, there is a need to be discrete and sensitive, for example, not taking notes in a face-to-face meeting when sensitive and/or personal information is being discussed or not taking notes too early on or too vigorously. But unless you are in the CIA or in a special selling situation such as international private banking in which your notes may compromise your clients, get out that note pad!

One of the great advantages of telephone selling is that you can take detailed notes unobserved. It would be a waste not to take advantage of this. From the minute you start talking on the telephone you should begin to complete a client contact form—*not* a scrap of paper. This form can be a file card or a notebook—whatever *system* you have to record the information you will need to maximize business opportunities now and later.

As you listen to your clients, write down more than numbers or technical information. Jot down key words, ideas, client interest, facts, neon words, wide words, questions, preferences, concerns, feelings, and personal information, such as vacation information, secretaries' names, spouses' names, the names of children, and important dates. All these can prove invaluable to you during the telephone call and later.

During the telephone call, as you jot down the client's key words or ambiguous phrases that need to be clarified such as "flexibility to grow," "worried about our subsidiary . . . ," "We don't care about having everything under one roof," you can hone in on those ideas. Take notes of what clients like and don't like and *why,* so that you can bring ideas to clients that mesh with their strategies, needs, and objectives. Transfer the information to the most accessible place; for example, once you get your client's secretary's name, put it on your rolodex and use it. Writing things down also increases the likelihood that you will follow up. When you say you are going to do something, say, "Let me make note of that . . . ," as a way to ensure that you *will* follow up and indicate to the clients that they can depend on you.

Every time you speak with a client, make it one of your objectives to learn something you can use. Of course, depending on importance and company policy, you may need to weed out a lot of information from your permanent file after the deal or sale is closed.

Take advantage of notes to prepare for your next call. Refer to your notes before making your next call to a client so that you don't waste precious time rehashing points already covered. Your smart clients are doing so and will not hesitate to say to you, "But Bill, my notes of April 5 . . . " *Be on top of things.* Notes help you clarify points later on should the client remember things differently from you. When a client says X and you know that you agreed to Y, it can be very useful for you to refer to your notes and say, "John, in my notes from June 4 . . . "

You can use the information in your notes to help you tailor your proposals and compose letters that reflect the clients' needs and interests — the clients' key words. One top producer asks clients, "What would you like included in the proposal?" and then uses his notes to tailor categories and develop information for his proposals. One client complained that a sales representative from a well-known company was lazy. Why? After three meetings the representative presented a *generic* proposal! Perhaps know-how rather than laziness was this salesperson's problem.

Once we were asked to team up with a much larger training firm to do one piece of a training package that, with the exception of this piece, was out of our field. We all met with the client for 3 hours and jointly decided that the two companies would develop separate, but coordinated, proposals. During the meeting we vigorously took notes; our colleagues from the other firm barely jotted down more than three lines — dates, a point or two. Two weeks later we all met. When the other firm presented its proposal the client expressed dissatisfaction. The boiler-plate proposal reflected little, if any, appreciation of the strategy and goals the client had presented so painstakingly during our joint meeting. The firm was asked to rework the proposal. We all met one week later. Again, a generic proposal was presented. Although the principals had contorted sections of the proposal, they did not pick up the "language" of the client. In frustration, their misunderstood customers, more tolerant than most, revised the proposal themselves. Even that didn't do the trick! The project continued to get stalled because our colleagues weren't listening. Eventually the whole thing fizzled.

Note taking is a mindset. Better note taking and better use of notes could have prevented this problem. With good notes, our colleagues could have easily developed a proposal that reflected the clients' thinking and structure. For example, they could have begun the proposal with the three objectives the client laid out (over and over) and then related solutions to the objectives.

Taking notes is a part of a relationship system that allow you and your organization to deliver quality service to your clients when you are not personally available. A colleague who has information on a transaction, for example, often can be helpful to the client in your absence. Also, if you circulate notes, a colleague who also works with the client can say, proactively, "I understand you are talking to Bill about . . . We are really doing great things. . . . How's it going?" This kind of support certainly is more professional than having the client think one department doesn't know what the other department is doing or having a colleague undermine your sales effort by saying, "Oh, I didn't know they were talking to you about that," or, worse yet, protectively saying, "I hope they are not bothering you."

11
Skill: Positioning Product

Questioning, listening, and, of course, homework will help you develop the information you need to *position* your story so you can tell it from your client's point of view. Positioning is truly the super skill. By knowing the client's perceptions, preferences, and needs you will be able to craft your product or idea accordingly. Even clients who have a commodity mindset can be helped to recognize differences if you relate your product to their specific needs. In the past, salespeople could count on the product to be the differentiator, but it is the fit with the client's needs plus the value added (quality, service, experience) that differentiates today. Even sales organizations determined to be on the cutting edge of every product need to make such differentiations clear to preserve price and market share, since competitors are adept at copying their unique product advantages quickly.

Positioning is more challenging when selling by telephone. In addition to missing body language and visual responses, you don't have the benefit of other cues, such as your client's office, with its tell-tale desk, photographs, decor, and level of organization. You have to compensate for this with skills and additional homework. But you can get information from other sources. For instance, with a little extra homework you could ask a colleague to tell you about the client and how he or she likes to get information. One sharp salesperson who wasn't getting too far with one client decided to ask for feedback from a colleague in the client's organization. The colleague said that although the client was impressed with the salesperson, he felt he was getting too much background. Since the colleague was being so open, the salesperson decided to press on. He asked, "How do you think I can correct that?" The insightful colleague replied, "You tend to give a lot of commentary. He just likes the bottom line." In a subsequent meeting the salesperson listened more attentively and became more aware of the client's short, to-the-point style of communication. But, more important, he was able to curtail the "whys" and "background," give short responses, and check for questions. Not surprisingly, there were none. The client really did not want *any* level of detail. When the salesperson finally met the client face-to-face, the client's level of formality further reinforced how to position information with him. Of course, it is not always possible to get the kind of insightful coaching described here, but many salespeople miss opportunities that help them position because they don't ask.

Product knowledge plays an important part in positioning. Because of the complexity of many products today, salespeople often need to use specialists to add expertise. Although team selling can be extremely effective, it doesn't exonerate generalists from developing at least a working knowledge of their key products or making sure they don't turn things over to a specialist prematurely. Essential as it is, product knowledge can be the crux of some salespeople's sales problems, and, sometimes, the better the product, the greater the temptation to do product dumps. The first and most important sales "rule" is to know the client's situation and needs *before* talking product. And then use the features and benefits that are relevant to the client.

Products are described through features (what the company puts into the product) and benefits (what the client gets out of it). Salespeople need to link features and benefits to sell effectively, but they must go further. Straight feature/benefit selling is product selling. As noted earlier, product selling won't carry the day, since product stories sound alike competitor to competitor. To position your product, although you may master a comprehensive list of features and benefits or bring along a "master" (specialist), you should tell the client only the part of your product story that *counts for the client.*

One salesperson avoided a product dump, although his client actually invited one. The client said, "We need something new. We need to change how we do X. Tell me what you do." The salesperson responded, "Yes, I appreciate the chance to tell you about our . . . and give you examples of . . . , since we have . . . experience. . . . But you mentioned the need for a change. Can you tell me what's happening to make you want to change, so I can understand better what it is you need to do?" "What are you looking for in the new . . . ?" With this information the salesperson was able to hone an otherwise laundry list of features and benefits, extracting and tailoring ideas and solutions that fit the client.

A different sales rep was not so skilled and got trapped into presenting a long list of features and benefits when she was selling to an engineer. The sales situation was a simple one, but the root of this problem is all too common to all kinds and sizes of sales. When he asked, "Why should I get a credit card with you?" she responded with a product answer—"We have 24 benefits." He challenged, "List them." Under stress, she recited 22. But the engineer didn't buy. Why? What he got was a product dump in which everything blended into something else, with nothing getting emphasis. The rep might have said, "We offer an excellent card with many benefits such as (give one). . . . So that I can focus on the benefits that would be of interest to you (*preface*), may I ask you a few questions?" Such a rapport comment and a question could have helped her sell the engineer by giving her an indication of his real level of interest. At the very least, it could have saved everybody time.

Sometimes you will be in the fortunate position of having clients or prospects call you and inquire about your services. This seems like a ready-made opportunity to tout what you can do, but asking some questions first to get more details can be enormously helpful. This, of course, will allow you to position, and there are other advantages to stepping back: It lets the client know that you are truly interested in what he or she *needs*. Because you don't "unload" information, you will be able to differentiate yourself from the other firm this client may also be calling. For example, in our company, prospects often get our name from a training directory that lists us along with about a dozen other firms. Callers say, "Send us information on . . . " or "Do you offer . . . ?" Although it is tempting to start telling, we find it very effective to start selling by asking instead. A reply like, "Yes, we do offer . . . for example. . . . But to help me understand your specific requirements, may I ask some questions? . . . " Callers almost always seem surprised and impressed when we ask detailed questions about what they need, for whom, what they have now, and where in the process they are.

As a salesperson, whenever you get stuck or caught short, it is very helpful to draw on the big three: *rapport, questioning,* and *positioning*. Unfortunately, most salespeople do just the opposite. Instead they *tell,* and this often takes them further away from the client. Positioning enables you to personalize, tailor, and get into a flow with the client.

To help you position your product as you sell over the telephone:

- Play devil's advocate before you pick up the telephone and ask yourself "What's in it for the client?"

- Come up with *three* compelling reasons why this client might be interested in your product. But remember to use the reasons *one at a time* and to check (question) before and after each one.

- Do your homework on your clients and their organizations—begin to identify their business and nonbusiness needs.

- Know your features and benefits so you know what you are talking about.

- Ask "open" need and strategy questions so that you will understand the client.

- *Listen!*

- *Tailor* your statements and questions to the client you are approaching. An engineer may want to know details on how things work, but a purchasing manager may want to focus more on price and warranties.

- *Personalize* your messages as well. Ask questions to get specific information on each client's approach and style.

- Use your total offer (*core* and *value-added* features and benefits).

- Know your objective. For example, if you are an institutional salesperson, ask yourself if this is a call to do a trade now or a call to build the relationship for a trade in the future?

- Plan your action step — know what your follow-up plan is and initiate it.

- Use your features and benefits one at a time (at most two at a time) and check for feedback.

- Use benefits *early* or your client is likely to say, "Listen, I've got to go."

- When you don't have an answer, say, "Let me look into that. What specifically . . . ? When . . . ?"

- Be selective. You have *limited* time over the telephone, so select key features and benefits and present them with an eye toward what the client wants to do.

- *Link* features with their benefits by using words such as *which means* and *so that* to bond features with benefits ("feature" *which means* "benefit").

- *Listen* to what your clients say and *incorporate* their ideas into your responses.

- *Take notes* as you listen so that you can incorporate your client's words now and again *later*. But don't repeat inflammatory words such as *"absurdly* low trade-in figure" which may further reinforce a misperception.

- Listen to the client's voice. Read between the lines and adjust.

- Speak your client's language.

- Avoid jargon unless you are talking to another "pro." Jargon is a great shorthand only if everyone understands it.

- Match the clients' level of sophistication — avoid talking down to clients or talking over their heads.

- Be accurate in the information you provide, but don't wait until you have perfect information. Let your clients know when your information may be imperfect, but also let them know you care about giving *timely* information.

- Choose your own words selectively. Avoid phrases such as "You *wouldn't* be interested in . . . " or "I'm *just* calling about . . . " Instead, use persuasive, confident words.

- Avoid the term *product*. It is better to say, "We have a way to increase interest . . . " rather than, "We have a product called _____."

- *Check* — ask for feedback, keep the dialogue going, get a measure of how you are doing *throughout* the call, especially since you don't have the benefit of reading the clients' facial expressions to gauge their reactions. Keep checking. Keep asking, "How does that sound?" Get feedback.

- Keep a positive attitude — remain helpful.

12
Skill: Checking

Checking lets you get feedback from your client on what you are discussing—while you are discussing it. Checking means asking questions to gauge your client's reactions as you go and is an essential skill in telephone selling, since you can't see your client's reactions. Checking helps you avoid waiting until the end of the call, if even then, to find out where your client is.

Telephone salespeople always say they need help in knowing how to read their clients. Checking is a practical and accurate way to get that reading without being expected to read a client's mind. By asking checking questions such as "How does that sound?" or "What do you think of that?" you can get the feedback you need to determine what to do or say next. In addition, the feedback helps you tailor your ideas to match up with the client. The process of checking will help you gain information and develop a dialogue with your client. But, in spite of these benefits, of all the six critical skills, checking is the one that salespeople *initially* resist most. Before they give checking a determined try, many salespeople say it seems canned or unnatural or that it makes them feel awkward. Actually, it doesn't come naturally for most people, but once the skill is developed, it becomes indispensable—a virtual secret weapon. One high-powered manager was so intent on making it a part of his selling process that he printed the word *checking* on a Post-It and stuck it to his telephone as a reminder.

Without checking, salespeople can make points but they fail to find out if the points *scored*—what the clients think of their points and how close the points have taken the clients to closing.

Checking means asking your client questions *throughout* the call to get direct feedback on what you just said. It keeps the dialogue going. For example, "How does that answer your concern?" lets you know if you have satisfied an objection. If a client says, "I'm still concerned about . . . " you can go over that necessary ground. Checking can also give you a "green light" to move on to another point after you *have* answered an objection or question. Checking helps you nail points down and focus. One salesperson missed an opportunity to advance in the sale when his client said, "Well, with X (competitor), I can talk directly to the trader." The salesperson replied, "Well, you can meet and talk to our trader in New York, too." While his suggestion was a good one, he got no mileage out of it. He simply just let the idea float in mid-air. He did not *check* and nail it down with an action step. Instead, he sailed on to his next point. Had he asked, "How does that sound?" followed by, "When would it be convenient for you . . . New York?" and confirmed an answer, he could have met a client need and moved the sales process forward a notch.

Because it gives you a reading on how the client is responding, checking helps you know when to close and when *not* to close. After you have discussed the point and you understand why the client really is not interested, *you* can be the one to say, "At this time this does not look right for you." Candor on your part, when both you and the client know the client is not interested, will be respected by most clients and will increase your credibility with them. This acknowledgement can save valuable time for you and your client and often gives you the chance to open up new opportunities—"So that I can look into it here, what *is* a priority for you now?"

Sometimes clients will reject the close or refuse to take the next logical step at the conclusion of the call in spite of having given positive feedback all along. In situations like this, checking gives you ground to stand on so that you can find out what is wrong and why things seem inconsistent. You can use the previous feedback as your rationale for asking about the client's reluctance to act in spite of positive feedback. You can say, "Tom, since we've discussed the . . . and how it could reduce . . . may I ask what concerns you have about . . . ?" Your goal is to uncover what is troubling the client while you are still on the line and have a chance to fix it.

As you check, listen to more than the words the clients use as they respond; listen to how the clients say the words. Listen for things like emphasis and hesitations, enthusiasm or flatness. Observe with your ears—interpret everything, including silences. If you sense the affect doesn't match the content, check further by asking another question. Based on the feedback you get, you can position what you say next.

Don't confuse checking with a high-pressure tactic or with manipulation. Checking questions are open-ended—what, when, how, to what extent. They are not designed to box clients into a corner—to force them to say yes. Many salespeople ask questions that are designed to guarantee a yes—"Don't you want to save money?"—the logic being that such a question will keep the client on the line and start a series of yes responses. Checking is *not,* "Don't you agree this benefits you by . . . ?" It is not, "Don't you want to save money?" or "Don't you agree?" These forced yes questions may have been effective in the past when clients were not as sophisticated about products and when there were far fewer options or competitors. The question for today's client is, "May I ask why is that?" or "How does that sound to you (after you present a feature or benefit)?"

Checking is not a summary from you. It is not, "I think X is great for you." It is *not* what *you* think but what the *client* thinks that counts. Checking allows you to find out something far more important than what you think. It helps you find out what your client thinks! Checking is, "What do you think?" It is based on the premise that what the client may say is more important than what you say. Checking is, "*Why* is it you are not interested?" Checking seeks to ferret out *good* and *bad* news, because you need both kinds of information.

Checking is not designed to get the client to say yes. It is designed to get at what the client thinks—yes *or* no. Checking is an essential skill for salespeople who want to know, really know, their clients' needs and how well they stack up to meet them. It is designed to get good or bad feedback so that the salesperson can position and close.

Of all the skills, many salespeople have the most trouble with checking. Yet there is no skill more helpful in giving you a measure of where you are in the call, in helping you set your course for the close, or in creating the 50:50 dialogue you need to sell today.

13
How the Six Critical Skills Work Together

All six critical skills—presence, rapport, questioning, listening, positioning, checking—work together. They are interrelated. They form a skill set. It is hard to talk about questioning without listening. It is impossible to talk about positioning without questioning. They tie together. Yet each can be developed, like a muscle, on its own. The six critical skills are used in *each* element of the call—when you open, when you are building rapport, when you question, when you listen, when you talk about your ideas, when you resolve objections, and when you close—you are continuously using the six critical skills. The six critical skills are your communication tools. A weakness in any one of these six critical skills will lower your overall performance.

The six critical skills are your sales muscles; they provide your sales strength and flexibility. The key to refining these skills is first to isolate and develop each skill. Most people have at least one weak spot, but each skill can be developed and refined. Each of you already has everything you need to sell (skillwise) inside of you. All of us do. Training, books, coaching, self-evaluation, and self-coaching are ways to help you tap inside and develop these skills that are already there. No one can teach anyone to sell, but you, your managers, and your trainers can help you maximize the natural skills and talents you have.

In the past, sales was looked at as a linear series of four or five steps that were supposed to come in a sequence. In the past this worked because clients were willing to be more passive in the process — to listen and learn. It bears repeating once more that this is *not* the case in today's competitive environment. All salespeople know that today the idea of four or five steps doesn't make sense because that isn't what really happens in a sales call. For example, a client can object as you are opening or while you are closing. Selling is not linear. If it were, the clients would have to go through sales training, not the salespeople.

Let's look at an example from a telephone call in which the salesperson used the six critical skills to handle a difficult situation with a prospect.

> CLIENT: "I should tell you right up front I hate your firm. You are unethical."
>
> SALESPERSON: "I'm sorry to hear that. But I do appreciate your being up-front about your feelings. I've been here . . . for seven years. *May I ask what happened to make you feel so strongly?*"
>
> CLIENT: "Five years ago . . . Is that (so and so) . . . still there?"
>
> SALESPERSON: "I wish I could tell you. The circumstances you describe do sound bad. We have 1500 salespeople in this company. I believe most, I would hope all, are ethical. May I ask . . . Yes, I do know. . . . In 1986 . . . I'd like the chance to look into this and call you back. Even if you never do business with me, hopefully, I can at least change your impression of our firm. Will you give me a chance to look further into this and get back to you?"
>
> CLIENT: "Hmm! Well, I can at least hear what you have to say."

This, like all the other examples in this book, has actually happened. The salesperson in this example did many things well. He faced a difficult situation with confidence and know-how. He avoided the pitfalls — he didn't give up, he didn't become defensive, and he didn't side with the client against his firm. He maintained his confidence and presence. He asked a question to get more information. He listened. He used empathy. He positioned his response as much as he could, and he checked to see if he succeeded in opening the door. His follow-up revealed that the client had been wronged and the salesperson in question in the mean time had been dismissed. But the good news was that the new salesperson won a new, big client!

Now let's look at other important aspects of telephone selling: preparation and getting to decision makers.

PART 3

Preparing for the Telephone Sales Call

In telephone selling, a haphazard approach usually leads to haphazard results. To maximize your telephone time, it is essential to prepare.

Preparation calls for a disciplined system. Successful telephone salespeople start with a call list and develop a system for tracking where they are with each call. Some salespeople color-code their lists to know at a glance where they are with each account. Others go so far as to keep a 3-minute egg timer on their desks as a way to help them manage call time.

14
A Basic Telephone Selling System

The fundamentals of any effective telephone system include:

- For prospecting, a concentrated block of *time* that you dedicate to your calls, not just one call between other activities
- An objective for number of calls you want to *complete* (prospects you will actually *reach*) per day
- Your client or prospect *list* for the day—in priority order
- A well-organized desk and environment
- An *objective* (what you want to see happen) *for each call*
- A record of each call (client information, details, next steps)
- A tickler system to trigger actions and follow-up
- Homework

Hitting Your "Number"

Telephone selling is often mistaken for a numbers game. But it simply is not enough to be diligent in making calls. *Too many tele-*

phone salespeople are just calling—not selling. Some people think the *more* calls the better. In the category of "believe it or not," one "salesperson" called the president of a *Fortune* 500 company for more than one year (one call each month or so) with no luck in getting through to him. Finally, he got the president on the line and asked him about his interest in X. The president said he wasn't interested, and, as unbelievable as it may seem, with that the salesperson hung up. This salesperson was calling, not selling.

Although it is true that the greater number of calls the greater the potential, making calls is not the object. The goal is to *achieve your call objectives.* To keep prospect calls in perspective, it can help to distinguish four kinds of call outcomes:

- Not connected (you called but did not get through)
- Connected (you got through but not to the person you were calling)
- Completed (you reached the individual you called)
- Objective met (you achieved your call objective)

The only numbers that really count is the last one—calls are only valuable when they help you reach call objectives.

Attempted calls, connected calls, and even completed calls are the first step in reaching your objectives. If they are well-targeted, such calls are a valuable use of your time. To increase efficiency, some organizations use technology such as touch screens or automatic dialing. But technology can only save seconds. It cannot change the facts of life. In general it takes at least two times the number of "connects" to achieve "completion" with prospects. Secretaries may pick up, clients may be on another line or out of the office, and so on. So if your goal is to reach 12 prospects, you might have to make as many as 24 or more calls to reach your targets. Of these prospects (actually only suspects up to this point), only some will be interested—willing to move forward to the next step, such as having you send information to them or sending information to you.

Your Telephone List

A telephone list is key. Top performers invariably have one ready to go *before* they start the day so that unexpected problems don't *keep* them off-track. They also review their lists at the end of the day and create a daily summary sheet to keep track of their activities and results. They take notes, often on call client contact worksheets (see Fig. 14-2), to provide them with details of the call for future reference, follow-up, and documentation.

Whether your system is manual or computerized, it should provide you with a way to move fast and move forward. If you are in a heavy prospecting mode, by tracking your call results you can gain invaluable information about your strengths and your weaknesses. By examining how many clients you called per day, how many connects you made, how many clients and prospects were reached, and how often you achieved your objective, you can determine your hit ratio. The information will help you build on what is working and figure out alternative strategies and approaches for the situations where you are not succeeding. For example, you may find that a particular client or group of prospects is more receptive very early in the day or that your success ratio drops if you wait longer than 2 weeks following a mailing to contact a client.

Some salespeople work from a telephone list their organizations provide—for example, a list of all corporations of X size in a particular geography, present mortgage clients who are good targets for cross-selling, or an affinity group, such as dentists in a professional association. Other salespeople must generate their own list of prospects. Some sources of prospect lists are:

- Current clients (to penetrate or do cross-selling)
- Former clients or relationships
- Former prospects
- Database and purchased information

- Company receptionists
- Telephone books
- Local directories
- Reverse directories
- Newspapers and magazines (people mentioned in articles or advertisements)
- Journals, trade papers
- Research
- Courthouse—UCC filings provide information about borrower, type of borrower (for example, secured borrower), who banks the prospect, date of filing, credit relationship
- Professional advertisements
- Chamber of Commerce
- Professional directories (local, national)
- Clubs
- Signs on trucks!

Your Desk

Before you begin your calls, organize all the relevant information you will need so that you don't waste time—yours or your client's. Have the information you need at fingertip reach—including reference books, brochures, and documents. For example, one sales manager requires all his *new* sales and trading generalists to use data and books that provide a historical perspective. In addition to such market information, make sure you have on hand data on the client or the target group you are calling and competitive information.

Clear your desk of extraneous papers. By organizing your environment, especially your desk, you can help yourself be more focused. Before you begin your call, be sure you not only have client and reference information handy but also any "aids" you need – calculator, paper, pens, and pencils. If, during a telephone call, you complete a contact sheet on a client or prospect and you don't want to file it because you plan to call the client back that day, use an accordion file with sections A to Z to save time, rather than let active contact sheets pile up on your desk. Be sure you use a consistent way of alphabetizing names so you know which letter to dive for when you are ready.

Your Environment

In telephone selling, since the other party cannot see you, it is easy to become distracted and focus on things apart from what your client is saying. You may have someone else on hold, on your mind, or at your desk. You may be running behind. You might even begin to read something that is on your desk or think about something that pops into your head. Your clients have similar distractions. Although such distractions are bound to occur, you need to concentrate on your client. As mentioned, your clients can sense when you are not listening to them, and they don't appreciate it. They expect and deserve your attention, especially when you initiate the call.

It is up to you to set your attitude and arrange your environment so that you can concentrate. Start by setting a block of time aside to focus on your list and accomplish your objectives. Whether you are making several calls or a series of 30 or more, make a commitment to achieve your objectives. Once you reach your client, pay attention! Stay tuned in! Listen, question, tailor what you say, take notes, and be aware of your voice and tone. If you begin to drift away, remind and tell yourself you are out of flow and get back into it. When your environment is not conducive to a concentrated effort, do what you can to change it. For example, arrange to use an office for important calls.

Prime Time

The concept of prime time is important in telephone sales. Prime time is the time when you can *reasonably* talk to clients. Prime time should be used to call and sell, and this can vary by product and target client group. Prime time is *not* the time to develop a list, do homework, write letters, have lunch, make personal telephone calls, chat with friends, or carry out any other support sales activities. It is not the time to read the paper or trade journals or do industry homework. When prime time starts, so should you!

There are levels of prime time, and in each industry these are different. The most important hours often need to be jammed-packed with priority calls. The time surrounding the "hot" time can be used in a less hectic way to make more in-depth, need-identification calls or support calls. When you are not in "hot" time, you can slow things down and take the time to uncover needs, learn about the client's longer range strategy, plans, and get feedback. As you prepare for each call you need to identify what kind of call it is. Is it a 3-minute do-a-deal call or a call to uncover needs and understand the client's strategy?

To maximize prime time, block out segments of time for your calls, ranging from one hour to the full day. Your prime time should be carefully guarded and maximized. For example, in financial markets the early morning calls are crucial, so you need to be very selective about who gets these calls. One high performer has a 1-minute timer on his desk to move him on to the next client after each quick presentation of market information and an idea for a trade. He appreciates that both he and the client he is calling have only a limited amount of time early each day and he shows that he values that time. In many telephone marketing centers—both those that market relatively simple products like credit cards and those that are selling complex mutual fund investments—salespeople are given time limits of 3 to 5 minutes for completing each call. As long as the amount of time is based on research, and salespeople are given both the training and flexibility they need to maximize their time, time limits can be helpful. Of course, this must be monitored for success and client satisfaction. Are goals being met? Are clients getting the information and service level they value? Not so for the salesperson who didn't qualify or check. He sent information that was totally inappropriate. Taking a little more time to ask questions might have changed that.

Telephone Call Objective/Purpose

Developing your list, choosing the right time to call, and creating the right sales environment to call are all good initial steps. But the most important step you can take is setting a *performance objective* for each call. As mentioned, your objective in telephone selling is what you want to accomplish by the end of the call. Do you want to get an application? Do you want a time for a next call with your client and his boss? Do you want to get an agreement to do business? In other words, what it is you want *the client to do* at the end of the call?

Most people do not set objectives that describe the *end* result they want. A performance objective spells out what it is you want to happen at the end of the call. Performance objectives can range from introducing an idea, to getting an appointment, to closing the sale over the telephone. None of these accomplishments is likely to happen if it is not planned. Performance objectives help you close, too, because they set an action step in your mind. Unless you set very clear measurable objectives beyond the vague one of "selling" — or, vaguer yet, "marketing" — you may find yourself doing more calling than selling.

These performance objectives force you to spell out what you want to see happen. They are measurable: They let you, or a dozen observers, for that matter, evaluate at the end of the telephone call whether the objective was achieved. At the end of the call you can say, "Yes, I got it" or "No, I didn't."

Performance objectives help motivate and "pathfind" all the way to the close. Although the close is a point in the sale, it is also a process that you begin before you pick up the telephone. Your performance objective is the first step in that process. Like a finish line to a marathon runner, the performance objective tells you where the destination is and how you are doing in getting there.

Of course, if you really want to achieve your objective, make sure it has value for the client too by positioning your objective to include *what's in it for your client* (your purpose). Your objectives generally represent what *you* want. But, as you set your objective, you also must think about your *purpose* — what the *client* wants. Think of your objective as a coin. It has two sides — an objective and purpose which make for a "win-win." The purpose is the *benefit* to the client. It answers the all-important question, "*What's in it for this client?*" Make sure you know the answer to that question *before* you pick up the telephone. And test your purpose — continuously. Since time is short on the telephone, lead early with your purpose to capture the interest of the client.

One final word about your objective and purpose — use them as tools not as handcuffs. Listen to your client and make adjustments based on your client's priorities and interests. Know how to refocus when need be and, of course, how, at the right time, to get back to your agenda.

Although your objective helps you set your focus, you need to know when to scramble your game plan. Whether your client has a different business priority, a personal problem, or simply does not have time to talk, be sensitive and flexible so that you adjust your plan. If the client says, "It's not a good time to talk," unless it is an urgent situation (a window of opportunity that will close), say, "Yes . . . , what . . . is there something I can do (which might give you information on what is going on). . . . When should I get back to you?" If there is a problem, be empathetic.

One new associate was inflexible with his agenda. He needed more help with his rapport building and empathy than he did with his objective-setting. Remember the young associate who set a performance objective to have the client swap X for Y? But when his client said, "This is a bad time to talk. My wife just called me and told me our daughter just dropped out of school," the associate said, "Don't worry. She's smart. She'll go back," and then he tried to continue into his pitch! No amount of preparation, no product knowledge, could compensate for this young associate's lack of empathy and poor listening skills. He was so focused on *his* objective that he missed a golden opportunity to help solidify a relationship by showing feeling for the client. Instead the associate charged ahead with his objective. Needless to say, he didn't get far.

Some clients will change topics or jump from topic to topic because they are not "organized" or possibly to avoid making a commitment or disclosing information. However, a clear picture of your objective and agenda can help you control such clients. For instance, if a client gets diverted telling you about an unrelated topic or complaining about a general topic not directly related to your objective/purpose/agenda, you don't have to get swept away. After listening, reflect on your objective and ask the client a question or make a statement that gets back to a discussion to test how serious your client is. Although you have to be sensitive and use your judgment, you can gain valuable information about your client's level of interest by gently, when the client takes a breath, leading back to your agenda to see what happens. Although some clients who waste your time give you business, most clients who really waste your time don't!

If your client mentions something as you and the client are discussing a point, you can acknowledge the point ("Yes, let's discuss X after . . . "), tactfully table it, close on the topic under discussion, and *then* pursue that point. Unless the products are interrelated, close on the first point first so you don't muddy the water and risk the first sale.

Homework

Do your homework. Be sure to review your notes from the last call to make sure you are not on the wrong track or representing an idea you already presented. Don't unwittingly use your precious time to present irrelevant or old ideas. Homework can help you set objectives that mesh with your client needs. Clients don't want their time wasted with irrelevant ideas or products. *Before you pick up the telephone, set your objective.* Set your agenda. Then check the agenda with the client. Ask, "What areas would you like

Client: _____ Contact(s): _____ Date: _____ Time of Call: ____

<u>Call Preparation Worksheet</u>

- Idea/Product:

- Client Needs:

- Decision Maker(s):
    - Key Economic Decision Maker(s)

    - Influencer(s)
- Your Client's Strategy:

- Call Objective/Purpose:
    - Objective

    - Purpose (What's in it for the client?)

- Questions to Ask:

- Anticipated Objections/How to Resolve:

- Key Features and <u>Benefits</u>:
    - Opening (Market Color/Hinge/ Referral)

    - Idea/Benefits Tailored to Customer

- Sales Team:
    - Roles

- Action Step:

c.c. _____, _____

Figure 14-1. Call preparation worksheet.

Call Client Contact Worksheet

Client: _____ Secretary's Name: _____

Organization/Company: _____ Telephone, Fax #: _____

Date: _____ Salesperson: _____

THE CALL

CALL AGENDA ITEMS:

-
-
-
-
-
-

CALL NOTES:

Information:

Needs/Priorities:

Time Frame:

Interpersonal:

NEXT STEP:

- cc:

(USE COLORED PAPER FOR CONTACT SHEET, I.E., BLUE TO STAND OUT ON A DESK.)

Figure 14-2. Call client contact worksheet.

to cover?" or "In addition to X, is there anything else you'd like us to cover?" Often clients will help structure and define the agenda.

Write down your agenda for the call and set it before you— even if it is a few bulleted points. It is easy to forget topics you want to cover, points you need to clear up, and so on; without a list you may find yourself making calls in which you are *not* maximizing your time or your client's time.

Because it is so easy for clients to disengage when on the telephone by saying things like, "I have another call," "I have someone with me," or "I'm busy," or to have their secretaries say, "She's not available," "He's on another line," and so on, be prepared to maximize each call when you do get through. Have relevant, tailored ideas lined up to present. Know your clients, their industry, their business, their needs, and the market, and align your objective so you can make headway.

Figures 14-1 and 14-2, preparation and client contact sheets, respectively, can be used for preparing for a call and for taking notes during a telephone sales call.

15
Telephone or Face-to-Face?

Once you know your objective, it is important to consider whether using the telephone is the best strategy. Although in many situations the telephone is the best strategy, in others it most definitely is not. Factors such as size of deal, economics of the sale, complexity, time frames, distance, importance, state of the relationship, whether you want to escalate or minimize the situation, standards in your industry for what clients will or will not buy over the telephone, client preferences, the product, the numbers of clients to be reached, and so on—all help determine the choice of telephone versus face-to-face. Some situations are clear cut. Others are not. Some salespeople need to decide when to go face-to-face and when to opt for the telephone and how much of each. Some businesses primarily rely on face-to-face contact for selling; others exist primarily on telephone sales. But most businesses today demand a healthy dose of both.

Knowing when to pick up the telephone or jump in your car, board a train or a plane, or write a letter or fax could mean the difference between winning and losing a piece of business. One equity telephone salesman switched from his normal strategy of telephone selling to making a face-to-face call. He had gotten a solid week of resistance from clients on the new product he was selling. He arranged for his product specialist and himself to *visit* with one of his key clients to get feedback and discuss the client's concerns with the product. Many of his colleagues facing the same resistance continued to make calls, griped, or backed away from the product—approaches that got them nowhere. However, by going out and meeting with a client and involving the product specialist, this creative and flexible salesperson was able to identify and fix the soft spot so he could "print" (close a sale).

In another situation, the president of a large paper company learned that he lost a million-dollar client because of how his company handled a pricing increase. The sales rep *faxed* a price increase to his 10-year, important client. The client faxed back saying they would pay only 50 percent of the increase. The sales rep responded by faxing that the first price was firm. Finally, the fax war stopped when the client telephoned the sales rep to say he was getting competitive bids, and the salesman needn't bother to fax any further. When the shaken salesperson advised the president of his company, the president immediately called the client, requesting a face-to-face appointment. Initially, the client refused. The president, a super salesman himself, asked the client about his satisfaction up to that point and proceeded to remind the client of all the special projects and needs that they accommodated for the client on a regular basis. He repeated his request for an appointment, but the client again said no. The president then took the client further down memory lane of very good service and accommodations. When the client again refused the face-to-face meeting, the president asked, "Will you reconsider in light of the past 10 years and let me call you tomorrow morning?" The client agreed. With this, the president felt 99 percent confident he could win the client back. The president attributes saving the account to (1) "begging," (2) his immediate responsiveness, and (3) accepting the 50 percent increase. The point of this story is the fax as the medium for negotiating was the *wrong* strategy. A telephone call could have saved time all around and avoided an unnecessary strain on a relationship.

Many salespeople primarily engage in telephone selling, for example, brokers, institutional sales and trading salespeople, and telemarketers. However, for big-ticket items when circumstances permit, it is very helpful for you to have met your clients so they have a face to attach to a name. A meeting helps personalize the situation. A telephone call can give you a few minutes, but with a face-to-face call you can have a minimum of 20 minutes and usually up to an hour or more. Although this may not always be possible or practical, shaking hands, making eye contact, and setting a personal dimension to the relationship can be invaluable. Even *one* face-to-face meeting can help personalize the situation, because people buy from people. Of course having met the client is *not* a prerequisite to doing business as attested to by the large number of salespeople who have long-standing, profitable relationships with clients they have never met. Nevertheless, for big-ticket or complex ideas or products, having a face with a name can give you a considerable edge.

The telephone is often your best bet in the following situations:

- You need to reach a large audience.

- You have to respond minute-by-minute to the market or have other significant time pressures.

- Your relationship with the client is solid (the firm will give you a complete hearing and is not apt to "shop" the idea).

- Your clients are sophisticated, experienced—the product is not a first-time buy for them nor are they first-time buyers with you.

- The sale is not overly complex.

- You are up-selling or cross-selling to your client base.

- The sale is not a big-ticket item, or the sale is big-ticket but other factors make telephone selling the industry standard.

- The product fits in with the client's strategy.

- The sale requires both face-to-face and telephone contact.

The key is for you to decide if your objective can be achieved over the phone. To help you decide if the telephone is the right strategy, consider each of the four elements that make up the best strategy: right time, right place, right people, and right benefits.

Right Time. Right time involves time and timing. As for time, one bank did *not* win friends with its strategy to have its credit card marketing staff start their telephone calls to a yuppie target group in New York City on Saturdays at *8:00 a.m.!* Consider *when* to make your telephone calls. Right time considerations include such issues as who gets the early morning calls from the institutional salesperson or broker or what time to call a difficult-to-reach executive to avoid a formidable gatekeeper (i.e., what time a rep should make a call, for example, after 6:00 p.m. rather than during the day).

Although making a telephone sales call almost at *any* time is better than not making the call (the call reluctance syndrome, "It's not a good time to call," is a real problem), the right time and good timing can give you an edge. Timing involves such things as knowing when in the sales cycle or in the relationship to do something or see someone. For example, an insurance underwriter must gauge when to call a broker for a renewal. A call too early creates a risk that the broker will shop the contract. A call too late prevents the underwriter from accessing the situation, setting a price, and doing the groundwork needed to price it right.

Right time also means knowing when to be *proactive*. An investment banker religiously telephones all his accounts *before* and *after* every client board meeting to make sure he has a shot at all new developments. Retail bankers in a bank that outperforms its competitors in CD retention call their CD clients 2 weeks before their CDs are due to secure the rollover, extend the term, or at least plant the seed in the client's mind to renew with them. One smart bank calls customers who have mortgages with competitor banks 3 months before the mortgage becomes due, knowing that the competitors will call only 2 months ahead. (They extract mortgage data from loan applications which are completed by their own bank's prospects or customers.) Another consultant finds out when his competitors are presenting and then calls his clients immediately following the competitive presentation to touch base. He uses the call to get feedback and reposition himself if necessary. One telephone salesperson not only makes it a point to meet all his priority clients face-to-face, he also brings in his senior each time a new senior client appears on the scene because he knows senior power can help anchor a relationship and serve as a tiebreaker when needed at decision time.

The idea of right time also helps you set your pace. For example, there may be a fast, hectic pace for early morning market calls, but that tempo can slow down later in the day, making it possible to take more time to identify needs and discuss strategy. Unless salespeople with hectic calling schedules consciously slow down and distinguish different kinds of calls, they may inadvertently create a hurried, uncover-needs atmosphere of "hot" time calls, preventing them from really getting to needs. An introductory comment like, "Now that . . . , I'd like to take a few minutes . . . if you have a few minutes . . . " can help change the pace.

You need to use your judgment and experience to determine precisely what the right time and timing means to you for your clients, and right time and timing often vary by product, client base, market, and so on. To determine when the best time is, use research, ask colleagues with more experience, use your own judgment and experience, *and don't forget to ask your clients and prospects* what their preferences are: *When does this client like calls? Meetings? How often? What is the best time of day or budget cycle to call or call back?*

Right Place. The phrase the *right place* gets to the heart of the telephone versus face-to-face choice. A telephone call creates a kind of meeting "place," but the question is, is it the right one? Even when the telephone is usually the right medium, sometimes face-to-face visits are essential.

Let's first look at a situation in which telephone selling, normally the right approach, did not turn out to be the best alternative. One newly assigned salesman made a choice when, after reviewing his *new* client's portfolio, he decided to make a radical recommendation over the telephone. He started off fine when he asked his client, "What are you trying to achieve with this group of stocks?" but he overstepped his boundary when he cavalierly advised his new client to sell 80 percent of his portfolio. Not surprisingly, the client did not respond well to such a recommendation from a *young* "stranger." The salesperson misjudged both the time and place. Within 1 week of this telephone call, the client called the sales manager of the firm saying, "The chemistry just isn't right." A new salesperson was assigned.

Fortunately, another salesperson did a better job of reading the situation. Although most of his business was normally done over the telephone, he opted for a face-to-face meeting because he was calling a *prospect* with a new hot idea. Since he did not have a relationship with the prospect, he was afraid if the prospect liked the idea, he would shop it. Even with the possibility of losing the window of opportunity, he decided to hold out for the face-to-face meeting. He limited his telephone call to introducing the general concept to the client and requesting an appointment. Since the potential benefits (indicative rates) he laid out grabbed the client's attention, he got a luncheon appointment for himself, his senior, and a specialist. In subsequent meetings they won an important and profitable piece of business. He held firm: "We've given a lot of thought to this, and we think it merits a face-to-face meeting." Now with that deal behind him, he regularly does business with this client—almost exclusively over the telephone.

Many salespeople use the strategy of calling a prospect or client in order to arrange a telephone sales appointment. Many clients say, "Now would be fine," but many appreciate setting the appointment for the phone call.

Right People.   Selling requires getting to the right people, but this is not always easy. Retail telephone selling provides the challenge of reaching the right party—for example, Mr. John Smith, Sr., not Mr. John Smith, Jr. In corporate or institutional sales the challenge of getting to the decision maker is greater and is compounded by gatekeepers. And when the organization you are calling is complex, even after you have who you think is the decision maker on the line, you may find you have an influencer or gatekeeper instead. Other times you may be speaking with the organizational chart decision maker only to learn (if you are smart enough to ask) that decisions are made by area heads under him or her or an administrative assistant who places the business.

Right people also means organizing the right people on your team. For example, you often have to orchestrate your teammates for a conference call or series of calls to peers on the client's side. Both activities require protocol and understanding client sensitivities. Some clients take offense at calls from a sales assistant or secretary rather than from their salesperson. Having a secretary call and ask them to "hold" for the salesperson does not rate much higher. However, there are strategies for dealing with these problems. Many successful salespeople facing severe "assistant resistance" make calls themselves, and note this on the rolodexes used by their assistants or secretaries. But to build up the role of their assistants, some include them in conference calls with clients. Making the assistants a part of the relationship gives the clients extra coverage and frees the salespeople up for their higher-potential clients.

One manager, as head of X, feels he has a better chance of getting through to prospects than his people do, so he uses his status to pave the way for his salespeople. He says, "It's then up to my people, but this strategy gives them a head start." (See Chap. 16, Getting to the Decision Makers.)

Right Benefits.   Everything about telephone selling tends to be faster, more abbreviated, and that is why it is essential to have relevant and compelling benefits on hand to use *early*. The right benefits can help keep clients and especially prospects on the line. Although you may be prepared for the call, clients or prospects usually are not. In most situations, they are not thinking about getting a call from you. Because your planned call can seem "spur of the moment" to them, the challenge is for you to set a focus, make them feel more comfortable, and gain their interest *fast*.

Using your homework on the client and the market, combined with your individual or organizational experience with your target client population, you should be able to line up several key benefits. By presenting these one at a time and early, you can capture the client's attention. But, no matter how confident you may feel about the "fit" between these benefits and your client, be sure to use the words "may" or "possibly" in positioning them. By doing so, you give yourself more leeway and add to your credibility. Of course, as you present these potential benefits, you should also get client feedback so that you can tailor your ideas to clients' interests.

Summary of the Four Rs

All four Rs — right time, right place, right people, right benefits — should be considered when you are determining whether telephone calling is the best way to sell in a particular situation. Let's look at how a managing director of a New York investment bank considered all four Rs to conclude that the telephone was the best means for solving a serious problem, although almost all his business was normally done face-to-face. His client, the owner of a major company, called on a Friday and threatened to back out of a deal on Monday if the bank did not meet his demand for the right to sell his shares of the company when the investment bank sold its shares. The investment banker did not jump into action. He waited for the *right time*. Since he knew the demand would be unacceptable to the investing third party, the managing director underplayed the problem by dealing with it over the telephone. He believed that a face-to-face meeting was not the *right place* to deal with the problem because it would *escalate* it; conversely, he knew the telephone could be used to minimize it. He further underplayed the problem by not dealing with it himself. He had a vice president in his group — the *right person* — call the client each day for 4 days to "soften him up," and then, in the afternoon of the fourth day, he called the client himself and expressed his confidence that the deal conferred the *right benefits* for the client — a strategy which was successful.

16
Getting to the Decision Makers

A major challenge of telephone selling is identifying and reaching decision makers. Of course it is usually more difficult to sell to decision makers in a prospective client situation than to sell to present clients. But even *reaching* clients can be difficult if your product is not a priority for them or if you or your organization are not on their "short list" of preferred organizations. Sometimes the sales environment or market can work against you and increase the difficulty of reaching clients. For example, after the October 1987 crash, as one broker put it, "Clients hid under their desks."

Even under less trying circumstances, clients may try to hide, and *gatekeepers* can help clients do this. Gatekeepers are the professional or personal screeners to protect clients' time. Getting past them takes grace and skill. They can work as a positive or negative force for you. Their professional roles span a broad range — managers, assistants, staff members, team members, colleagues, administrators, secretaries. On the personal score, a gatekeeper may be a spouse or any one who answers a home telephone.

In almost all situations, gatekeepers are a vital link to your ultimate client. They may not be final decision makers, but they can be powerful influencers. Underestimating their importance can be a costly mistake, because at all levels they can be the path to your final decision makers.

Your goal should be to align gatekeepers and turn them into allies. You have basically two options for dealing with gatekeepers:

- You can get gatekeepers' support and go *with* the gatekeepers (physically with them or with their blessing).

- You can go *around* gatekeepers (*without* them and *without* their support).

Certainly the level and power of the gatekeeper will help determine which strategy to choose, but, in general, choosing to go overtly around a gatekeeper is risky business. You may alienate the gatekeeper to the point you blow up the path to the ultimate decision maker. Also consider the probability that the gatekeeper, regardless of how weak an influencer at the present time, may rise and carry a grudge as he or she moves up. If, for example, you directly call the CFO or VP of Corporate Development against the directives of your contact, the treasurer, you risk losing the treasurer's support and create a formidable enemy. Also, the individual who functions as gatekeeper may actually have more decision-making authority than you think and may even be in a position to direct business to you or apprise you of opportunities. A *Fortune* 500 executive uses his secretary to place "buy orders" and lets her decide who to call and in what order. One of the salespeople on the account gets a disproportionate amount of business from this client because he knows to treat this secretary as the client.

Aggressively going around or over your gatekeeper when the gatekeeper is influential will more often than not backfire on you and is apt to have long-term negative consequences. It is a calculated risk. The only time overtly circumventing your gatekeeper makes sense is when you have nothing to lose and/or when you assess that the risk is worth it. For example, one computer salesperson was well-positioned to go around a gatekeeper: When his contact said, "It doesn't look like you are going to get this one," the salesperson, who knew he had a superior solution and price, took the president of the company up on his offer to get back to him if need be. The salesperson advised his contact, approached the president, and sold the largest account of the year for his company.

Even when you go around gatekeepers, you may face them again. Since the world is a small place, and having absolutely nothing to lose is rare, minimize conflict as much as possible. You can find elegant ways of achieving this such as:

- Bring in a senior.
- Have another department make contact.
- Call when the gatekeeper (your contact) is away.
- Say your senior has asked to meet your contact's manager.

Even using these tactics, be certain you have a very good product or idea, or the repercussions can be disastrous.

Despite the inconveniences and even dangers gatekeepers pose, they serve a valuable role for their managers and for you. After all, the same gatekeeper who can rebuff you can turn away your competitor, too! Don't think of them as a "necessary evil." Think positively!

Find ways to cultivate and win the support of gatekeepers. It takes a positive attitude, sincere respect, and effective communication skills to turn gatekeepers into advocates. You also must figure out "What's in it for the gatekeeper?" One of the best ways to accomplish this is to find out what the gatekeeper's objectives are and then line up what you can do to help the gatekeeper meet those objectives. Of course to find out nonpublic information, such as how people get their bonuses and promotions, requires having a close, open relationship with clients. If you can find a way to *help* gatekeepers, you will surely share in their success.

Some tactics you can use to help you work with professional gatekeepers and get them to support you are:

- First and foremost, give credit back—make sure the gate-keepers' seniors know how helpful or effective they are. Say positive things about gatekeepers to other people inside the client's company and say positive things about them to others in the industry—*it will get back to them.*

- Show them how they will benefit from your product or idea.
- Find out what's in it for them.
- Make *them* feel important.
- Call them frequently and early—*keep them informed.*
- Be sensitive in how you handle them, for example, send cover letters to them with anything you c.c. to them, don't just send them a copy.
- Ask for their ideas; ask them for their help; turn them into coaches.
- Be *helpful*—make their job easier.
- Be interested in them.
- Be polite and show respect for them (including them, looking at them also when you are meeting with them and the decision maker).
- Use their names.
- Thank them for their help.
- Take time to build rapport.
- Keep them posted of ideas/developments.
- Be genuine.
- Cultivate them early in their careers before they become powerful.

Working with Your Clients' Secretaries/Assistants

Some gatekeepers, especially executive secretaries, are very good at screening and blocking callers. The higher up the contact, the more efficient the screening and the greater the number of protective layers.

Secretaries often have the ear of the decision maker and can influence their thinking. Executive secretaries, as well as other secretaries, usually have the trust of their managers and, therefore, can shape their manager's perception of you. Once you have established a rapport with these secretaries, they can be invaluable sources of insights and important information about your clients. They can alert you to both opportunities and problems. One secretary told her favorite salesperson during a telephone call that it was the president's tenth anniversary with the company on the particular day that the salesperson was scheduling a lunch with him. The secretary also tipped the salesperson off to his favorite restaurant. Needless to say, the salesperson went ahead and reserved the president's favorite table, where the two celebrated in style. The president was touched by the gesture on the part of the salesperson and what was already a good relationship was strengthened.

A new salesperson was lucky enough to learn secondhand rather than the hard way how important it is not to alienate secretaries. He was waiting in a reception area when one of the secretaries seated outside the senior vice president's office answered the telephone. The secretary put the caller on hold and announced to the secretary sitting next to her, "It's X, that [expletive]. It's the second time he's called today. He's such a jerk. I hate it when he calls me 'honey.'" "Honey" let him keep "blinking" on the line. She didn't even bother to tell her boss that he was calling. After waiting about 3 minutes, the caller gave up and the telephone light went out—along with a potential opportunity.

One client actually stopped taking calls from a well-known consultant. Why? He was demeaning to her secretary. After giving the secretary a 5-minute message, this "superstar" consultant asked this exceptionally competent and helpful secretary to read his message back to him. She had not taken the message word for word, for example, she translated the consultant's "if X could not attend the luncheon, someone else should be *nominated* to attend the luncheon in his place" to read "if X can't go, send someone else." When she read the message back to him, the consultant said, "That's not what I said. I want you to take it word for word." He then repeated the lengthy message and again demanded she repeat it! This might have been justified if the message were highly technical or critically important. But without such justification, the consultant's approach was inappropriate. Certainly the message was important to the consultant and he was trying to be more persuasive by using the word "nominate." However, although the consultant finally got his message through verbatim, he got another message across: He was demanding, out of line, and off a major client's list!

Most secretaries will be helpful if you approach them in a professional and friendly way and, of course, if you can convince them that you have something of value to offer their manager. Once you establish a positive relationship with them, you will have far fewer problems, but, until then, getting by gatekeepers is a major challenge.

Some tips include:

- *Attitude!* Be polite and friendly while also being confident (not arrogant). Be genuine. Don't be condescending.

- Ask for their help: "Can you look at X's calendar . . . ?" Say, "I'd like to get to him. Can you suggest a time to call him that would be convenient for him?"

- Once you get the secretary's name, put it on your contact sheet and rolodex card or screen and *use* it.

- Make sure it is your prospect's secretary you are speaking to. Be sensitive to job titles, and, to be on the safe side, ask, "Are you Bob Sharp's assistant?" Some administrative assistants are offended if referred to as secretaries, so use the word *assistant*. The person who answers will tell you his or her role if you get it wrong. Women in management who are mistaken for secretaries do not appreciate the stereotype. If you think you may have reached a nonsecretary, it is better to err on the high side, asking "Are you with the X group (referring to your client's department or division)?"

- When calling a *prospect,* give the secretary only *one piece of information at a time.* Most secretaries instinctively will ask at least one screening question. Since you would probably prefer that they ask for your company's name than for the nature of your call, start by only giving your name. For example, "This is Tom Green, is he there please?" State your firm or institution when asked, unless you are in a business that bombards your market and clients with calls, such as brokerage. Then you can delay by saying, "Tom Smith's office calling." In another example, you are with a brokerage firm and the secretary says, "Mr. X does not wish to talk to brokers (you in the generic)," so you will have to find a way to extricate yourself from that group and its agenda. Separate yourself from the pack by saying something like, "I am not calling about a product. Mr. X knows my firm and I am calling to make a personal introduction." Once you state your reason, be silent and put the onus on the secretary for what happens next. Silence is a powerful tactic on the telephone. As you remain quiet the secretary will have to determine what to do next.

- If you get resistance—"He is very busy. May I help you?"—make a second effort, remain positive and polite, but again try to get directly to the decision maker. But when secretaries ask to help you or ask the nature of the call, be sure not to offend them by implying your call is too important for them or too complex for them to understand. Instead say, "Yes, I am calling about . . ." and provide a general statement such as " . . . an executive program for . . . that Mr. Smith will be very interested in . . . " and then add "I'd very much like to speak with him." Again, seek the secretary's help by asking, "When do *you* think I could get to him?"

- Use a *hinge* such as a personal referral ("Bill Tims said I should call.") or refer to a letter you sent, an article, and so on as a way to warm up an otherwise cold call. End your letters with the fact you will be calling so later you can truthfully say, "X is expecting my call."

- Tell the truth. If the secretary asks you, "Does he or she know you?" and you do not know the client, say so. Almost nothing is more annoying to the client than being tricked. To help you get through this objection in the form of a question you could say, "No, Mr. X does not know me, but he is familiar with ABC (your company)."

- Be persistent without being obnoxious. Know when to say it is "urgent"; don't cry wolf. Sometimes it is essential that you get through to your client. For example, when you are calling about a market-sensitive idea or product, you may need to get through immediately before the market moves. If the client is not available, whether she or he is on another line or out of the office, be resourceful. If you have not "cried wolf" in the past, you can say that there is a time pressure: "June, when can I get to him? The *market is moving* . . . opportunity . . . and I'd like to get to him as soon as possible." In most time-sensitive situations it is better to keep in control of the follow-up. *Do not* leave it up to the client to call you—especially on voice mail!

- Call back. If asked for it, leave your name and number to have the prospect call you back, but don't expect the call. Leave the door open for you to call. Say, "I may be away from my desk (or out of the office) often . . . , when can I call . . . ?" or "I will call . . . "

- *Call at lunch time, before 9:00 a.m., or after 5:00 or 6:00 when secretaries are less likely to be at their phones and clients are most likely to pick up their own telephones.* If a secretary does pick up at these times, depending on the situation, give a pat on the back. Say, "You're an early bird" or "You're working late!"

- Be genuine. Find your fine line between being too distant and being overly friendly.

- Build rapport. Use the secretary's name. Say "thank you" and "please." After you have spoken with the secretary several times, you might say, "Tom, it's Mary Smith. I hope you had a nice weekend (or "How is it going today?"). *Listen* . . . Is he there?"

- Be sensitive in how you address or refer to female secretaries. For female secretaries, don't use the word *girls* as in "When I spoke to your girl." If the secretary has passed puberty, she is a woman, so if you don't know her name or title but need to refer to her in conversation, do use the term "woman" or "young woman."

- Treat secretaries as intelligent people. Although you need not volunteer details, do give them fundamental information. Don't imply they are not intelligent, sophisticated, or trustworthy enough to handle the information.

- If the secretary is not very efficient, take more time in your conversations, be sure to follow up, and always put things in writing.

■ Send flowers, candy, cards, and so on for holidays. One successful consultant gives the same size box of fine chocolates to secretaries as she does to her clients at holiday time. Since most salespeople differentiate clients by gift, this can give you an edge. Certainly the secretary will appreciate it, and your client may, too. You can, however, give your client an additional gift.

17
Telephone Call
Formatting

Telephone call formatting is a process inexperienced salespeople can use to prepare for their telephone sales calls. It is also helpful for salespeople new to telephone selling and for experienced telephone salespeople who are selling a new product. The formatting process, which matches up with the telephone selling framework, offers an alternative to telephone scripts, which usually sound unnatural and stilted. The problems with scripts are (1) they are read and most often lack a "present" quality and (2) they are preset and standardized and offer no flexibility. Since few people, aside from professional actors, can capture the present tense in their voices, salespeople who read scripts kill one of the most valuable selling skills—presence. When that skill is down, all the others are doomed to go as well.

With a script there is no or little tailoring to the individual. Salespeople who rely on scripts often can't respond to questions and easily get thrown off course by interruptions. Scripts seem to take the humanity out of selling by forcing salespeople to become robotlike. It is much better for salespeople to use their own words—almost any words! But formatting can help you find the *best* process. Formatting provides the road map for the telephone sales call framework but allows you to fill in the specifics of the dialogue to match your personal style and your client's needs.

The elements of formatting match up with the elements of a telephone sales call. They are: opening, client needs, product or idea positioning, objections, and close.

Let's briefly review the six elements.

Opening

- Greeting
- Introduction
- Summary/hinge/referral

  Referral, letter, etc.
- Rapport
- Agenda (objective and purpose)

  Potential benefits *early*

  Check: Is this a good time to talk? (optional)
- Bridge to needs

Client Needs

- Check for client needs after you present your purpose and key benefits: "Have you looked at . . . ?" "How familiar are you with . . . ?" "How does that sound?"

Qualify

- If you are not sure if this client qualifies, ask qualifying questions.

Product Positioning

- Position your product to match the client needs.
- Engage in a dialogue.
- *Use checking throughout.* Determine what the client thinks of your idea/product as you discuss it.
- Based on your objective for the phone call, give as much or as little information about your product as appropriate. If your

Call Formatting Worksheet

Opening	OPENING	Remember

Opening
- Greeting and
  Introduction
  (Name,
  Company,
  Client Name)

- Rapport

- Summary

- Agenda/Objec-
  tive and Purpose
  (Benefit)

- Is This a Good
  Time to Talk?
  (Optional)

Client Needs
- Identify/Confirm
  Needs

NEEDS/RESPONSE TO NEEDS

Qualify

Product Positioning	Features	Benefits	Client Need

**Product
Positioning**
- Position Features
  and Benefits
- Questions --
  Respond to and
  Ask
- Checking
  - Check if
    there are any
    questions
- Use Your Total
  Offer

CLOSE

Close

- Ask for Business
  or Next Step
- Restate
- Say Thank
  You/Sign Off

Remember
The Six
Critical
Skills:

PRESENCE
- Voice
- Confidence

RELATING
- Courtesy
- Rapport

QUESTIONING
- Dialogue
- Needs

LISTENING
- Verbalize
  Responses
- Notes

POSITIONING
- Tailor Your
  Presentation
- Features/
  Benefits/
  Needs

CHECKING
- Get Feedback

Second Effort -- Objections

Figure 17-1. Call formatting worksheet.

objective is to get an appointment, *limit* the product discussion. If your objective is to close, a more full discussion is called for.

Objections

- Use the objection resolution model. (Note that this model is a floating element to be used whenever an objection is raised.)

Listen.
Give second effort or third!
Maintain your *presence.*
Show empathy by *relating* — repeat objection.
Ask *questions.*
Listen to the answers.
Position features and benefits matched to needs.
Check: Ask if client objections have been satisfied.

Close/Request Next Step/Action Step/Commitment

- Ask for the order or the next step.
- Restate (confirm and/or repeat agreement) and hang up — "Done. Thank you."
- Give a second effort (resolve objections).
- Sign-off: "Thank you. . . . "

Follow-Up

- Carry out the next step.

Figure 17-1 is a form new salespeople can use to format a telephone sales call by filling in ideas to use during the telephone sales call.

PART 4
Prospecting

18
Getting the Appointment

No sales book would be complete without addressing getting the first appointment with a prospect—a task considered by many salespeople to be the greatest challenge. A number of salespeople simply freeze up when it is time to make *prospect* calls. They dread the thought of them. Certainly hesitation is understandable. What lies ahead? Gatekeepers and prospects that are "too busy," "not interested," "already satisfied," and many who say not to call again in no uncertain terms. Yet other salespeople find it easy to be motivated to pick up the telephone and prospect for business. What is it they do that their less successful colleagues don't? Let's look at that first. Then we will look at how to deal with chronic reluctance to make prospect calls, how to make qualified appointments, and how to be more successful.

In looking at the salespeople who get appointments, we find they are "up." Their voices, their choice of words, their attitudes exude the confidence that says, "I have something of value." While some do admit, "If I'm not in a good mood, I don't even try," all really successful prospectors are in a "good mood" or up *most* days. Also, they are not thrown off by an unproductive (no-appointment) or unpleasant call or even a *series* of no-interest calls. They just keep going when their less successful counter-parts get discouraged. Salespeople not so successful in their pros-pecting efforts conclude too quickly that, "It's not a good day," or they find reasons not to get back to calling. There are tell-tale signs: the continuous delay and excuses for not picking up the phone and prospecting; a feeling of relief when the prospect isn't available to take the call; the extended lunch; the too-busy, no-time syndrome; the lack of a prospect list; no attempt to get re-ferrals. But the real tell-tale sign is that sales are no longer on the rise and production is leveling off. And the salesperson feels that he or she can do better. But salespeople who are really good at prospecting have a resilience that enables them not to get thrown and helps them bounce back when they are thrown. They look at the unproductive calls not as bad calls but as part of the process. They see these calls as "round one" and the next calls as "round two" and so on—they jump back into the "ring"!

It really is mainly a matter of attitude and experience. An atti-tude is what you know about something and how you feel about it. A good example of attitude can be seen when a child who has never tasted spinach "knows" he or she doesn't like it. And as any parent knows, attitudes can be very strong. Successful prospec-tors often have a good attitude about telephone prospecting, not so much because they feel naturally positive, but because they have had many good experiences. And, of course, they have *more* experiences because they don't quit and they probably have know-how. Attitude, experience, and skill reinforce each other.

Salespeople who succeed often describe themselves as being on a "roll," and when this happens they keep calling and keep suc-ceeding. One very successful sales manager who loves prospect-ing says he wishes he could "arrange" the first few prospect calls each of his new salespeople make. He feels if he could "set up" his "good" customers to take these first calls and agree to ap-pointments with little resistance, he would help his people de-velop positive attitudes about prospecting that would bring them future success. "These initial successes would pave the way for more," he says. Of course, no one is 100 percent successful, but a positive attitude and know-how helps increase the success ratio and insulates against the impact of rejection that comes with, as they say, "the territory."

Next comes skills. Successful prospectors are skillful. They use the six critical skills to build rapport, get through gatekeepers, and deal with objections. Successful prospectors also have an organized prospecting system. It is not hit or miss. They know their territory. They do their homework. They prioritize their prospect list. They set call objectives. They set a *block of time,* not one call at a time, and they don't get distracted. Then these prospectors use a multitude of approaches—telephone, mailings, even some "cold" calls (walking in *without* a prior telephone appointment) to maximize a free hour between appointment calls or in calling on very small companies.

Call Reluctance

Call reluctance is contagious. Salespeople are as vulnerable to it as much from bad example as a bad experience. Many sales trainers and sales managers promote the condition unintentionally because they dislike prospecting. Many new salespeople in our seminars start out with a mild form of call reluctance but develop a more severe case once they are exposed to colleagues suffering from acute cases. But when exposed to managers or colleagues who "love to call new customers," the cure can begin.

Before moving on to specific techniques for successfully making sales appointments with prospects, let's consider why so many salespeople are reluctant to call prospects. Salespeople who suffer from call reluctance most frequently give two reasons. First and foremost is the fear of rejection. Next in line is the desire not to intrude on people, not to be a pest. So they resist picking up the phone and asking to speak to a prospect or customer—either for an appointment or a sale. Most salespeople who are reluctant to call can help themselves. Of course, there are varying degrees of call reluctance, but the first step in self-help, as for all problems, is recognizing that there is a problem. When James Joyce, the great Irish writer, used the phrase, "The viability of vincinals are invincible when invisible," he meant just that—if you don't see the problem, you cannot fix it.

Let's look at the relationship between the two reasons—fear of rejection and not wanting to intrude. Actually they are linked.

The more skilled one is, the less one suffers rejection (of course there will always be some rejection). If, as a salesperson, you think you are intruding, you are likely to convey that attitude and make selling mistakes that will stimulate even more rejection. For example, you might say, "I'm sorry to disturb you" or quit at the first hint of resistance. Also, salespeople may associate the calls they make with the annoying phone calls they get at home—calls in which *they* are the ones who do the rejecting. But think about business customers. They have phones, and the essence of the phone is *interruptions*. Interruptions, however, are different from intrusions. There is a big difference. When you think about the things salespeople do who call you at home that *annoy* or aggravate you, you will likely see that your negative feelings stem from feelings of intrusions. Think about what bothers you: You are at home, and you consider your home a private place by invitation; but second and more important, you feel the caller (if you are annoyed by him or her) is self-serving and insincere. You can and should avoid both or at least the second of these negative factors in business calls.

Your customer expects phone interruptions. It is the nature of business. In a business situation these interruptions are acceptable; intrusions are not. You can avoid intruding by knowing how to call. Know-how can help you distinguish yourself from "hype" phone selling.

Senior management often says, "Motivate my people." Pep talks sound good. But often the hard-core reality of call reluctance remains after the echo of a motivational speech is gone. And salespeople who suffer from call reluctance feel worse because not only aren't they making the calls, they now are more conscious of their failings and are ridden with guilt.

Know-how and a disciplined system and positive mind-set are the answers to a fear of making prospect calls, as long as the salesperson *wants* to. The only salespeople who can't be helped are those who have low motivation and don't care about correcting the problem. If they are motivated and care, know-how can turn things around.

Reaching your prospects or customers can be a challenge, so by the time you reach them be ready to *sell* the appointment. Don't just call! Many salespeople are calling, not selling. Many seem surprised by rejection or nonplussed, and they say "okay" and hang up.

Recap of Framework for Getting the Appointment

Let's look at the framework to increase your success in getting a telephone appointment call with your prospects:

1. *Prepare.*
   - Prospecting begs for preparation. Do your homework, research files, ask around. Do homework on the prospect and identify the hot buttons in the industry and the company and person you are calling and make assumptions about which benefits to use.
   - Before you pick up the telephone, set a call objective (what you want to get out of the call) and consider the flip side of the objective, your purpose (what the prospect can get out of the call, how the prospect *might* benefit) and avoid hype. Visualize what you want and when you want it.

2. *Opening.*
   - Greeting.
   - Introduce yourself, your organization, and your group (just the name of your organization/division). Tell the name of your organization/division only. In a few moments you can tell those things about your organization or experience that are relevant and potentially beneficial to the customer. You should *not* explain who your organization is or what it does yet. Cover this when you get to your need/benefit statement.
   - Use a referral if you have one or any hinge, such as a letter or an article about the prospect, to warm up an otherwise cold situation.
   - Establish *rapport* through a friendly, upbeat voice. Be confident and natural in your tone and pace. Avoid any trace of exaggerated claims, hype, or arrogance. In certain areas (geography, culture, industry, and factors like time of day), avoid rapport comments that might be construed as

ingenuine or inappropriate ("How are you today?") but be sensitive to cultural differences in areas in which rapport comments are appropriate.

3. *Need/Benefit Statement/Agenda.* Keep in mind this is someone who does not know you. Prospects can and will disengage easily if they do not perceive a benefit relatively quickly. So using your homework and experience, be prepared to make *a need/benefit statement* not a self-serving statement. This will serve as a magnet to the prospect on the phone. The best magnet is to show prospects what's in it for them. In a sense, this need/benefit statement is your brief *commercial.* Refer to something about your area of expertise or product that you feel would interest the prospect and, if you have examples, then mention that you have been successful with X or Y (names that would influence your prospect). The potential benefit you mention can be general or specific depending on how much information on the prospect you have. The more specific—if you are sure—the better; the more specific—if you are not sure—the riskier. In any case, be prepared to ask why if the client says he or she is not interested, and, depending on the answer, have a backup benefit ready. Your "commercial" discusses the potential benefit to the customer and then uses the names of clients, mentioning your success in that area. This name dropping, tactfully done, will help establish your credibility. You could say, "We have done (benefit). For example, we worked with (repeat companies) and were *successful* in (tell briefly what you did and for whom). As you do this, keep a business tone and avoid all hints of exaggeration or outrageous claims. Absolutely avoid asking self-serving or leading questions (a question asked to manipulate and force a yes) such as "Don't you want to save money?" or "Do you want to increase productivity?" These questions can be insulting and aggravating to your prospects. Don't push your product with no concern about whether the prospect is interested. If the prospect is not interested, express empathy and then ask why. Have a backup benefit handy.

4. *Need Check.* Once you have made a need/benefit statement, check how interested the customer is. You are subtly asking for an okay to go further and expand on the need/benefit statement. One top salesperson says, "I got your name *as a key person in this area,* and I'd like to take a few minutes to discuss this to see if this is an area you are involved in or interested in" or "I was given your name as a key . . . Is this your area?"

5. *Time Check.* Ask if it is a good time to spend a *few* minutes. This is a gesture of courtesy. It is also a smart business thing to do, since choice reduces defensiveness. Your time check question must be asked after you have made your *need/benefit statement* so that hopefully you would have captured the interest of the customer. If it is not a good time, set a time to call back.

6. *Qualify (Semiqualify).* If you are absolutely sure you want to see this prospect — the prospect is "prequalified" by size, prestige, ranking in the industry, information on the prospect — you can forgo qualifying. But even then if the prospect seems open, you can get a bit more information to help you prepare for the call. If not, simply say you would like to "set an appointment to (restate the *potential* benefit briefly)" and ask for the appointment. However, if your prospect list is not prequalified, if, for example, you are calling smaller companies, or if you have a large number of prospects, tactfully qualify the prospect. However, keep in mind that in most situations this, at best, is semiqualifying, since with any attempt to fully qualify you may find that you talked yourself out of the appointment. As you qualify, you will uncover needs, so take *notes* (see the telephone contact sheet, Fig. 10-1) and use them to prepare for the call. In this process, be sure not to go into your sales call in any depth. If you need a face-to-face call, don't do much more than set the appointment on the phone. If you try to accomplish more than just getting the appointment, you won't *need* an appointment, and you probably won't get one. Your prospect may try to get you to get into the sales call, but you should keep your eye on the ball — go for the appointment. Tell prospects how a short meeting would benefit them — to understand their situation, tailor, etc. When you

need to qualify, do so. It will help you make sure it is worth your and your customers' time. At the same time, don't talk yourself out of the appointment by asking too many qualifying questions. Some topics to cover as you qualify are:

- Short and long-term goals
- Time frames
- Decision makers
- Preliminary needs
- Budget information
- Information you can use to prepare for your next contact/ face-to-face call

7. *Ask for the appointment* emphasizing a time that would be *convenient for the prospect:* "I'd like to get together to . . . " or "I'll be in . . . on . . . " A businessperson respects planning and is likely to think, "I wish my salespeople did that." It is a matter of style: You can ask for an open time frame—"I'd like to get together at your convenience in the next week," or "How about Tuesday?"—or take more responsibility by offering a date—"I'll be in . . . on Wednesday, April X. Would that be convenient for you?" If the prospect says, "No, I'm not here that day," or "I'm golfing," bounce back and say, "Well, what about Friday of the following week?" Depending on the customer's openness, you could use humor—"Oh, I play golf too. Where do you play?"

8. *Second Effort after Your Prospect Objects.* Even interested prospects object: "Tell me now . . . ," "I'm too busy," "I just bought . . . ," "I have no budget." Prospects are naturally cynical. They often suspect your motives. Most prospects respect and expect a second effort. They know you know they must guard their time, money, and information. *Make a second effort* by expressing empathy and then *ask a question*. Find out why. Use the objection resolution process: "Since we are seeing so much . . . may I ask why?" Tailor the benefit further, as much as possible, and then ask for the appointment again. The second time you ask for the appointment, *limit* the proposed appointment to *20 minutes,* and use the 20 minutes to

begin a dialogue and then determine if a full appointment is appropriate. This combination of the *consultative approach plus the 20-minute tactic* helps persuade the most reluctant prospect.

9. *Close and Confirm.* Wrap things up with these two steps: Confirm the appointment by repeating the appointment date, time, place, and your name; add, "For your calendar my name is X . . . " (and spell it), "thank you."

You can increase your success ratio in setting appointments if you understand the *process* for making a telephone appointment. This is a typical exchange:

"Hello, Mr. Patton. This is Ron Cooper from X." (Greeting, introduction, state the name of your company.)

"After reading about . . . in the *Wall Street Journal* . . . " (Hinge.)

"I thought I'd call because we have worked with companies like yours, such as A, B, and C Companies, to . . . (this can be general such as 'in helping them with their financing' or specific such as 'to speed up collections of,' depending on the information you have and your product line), and we have had *excellent results* (or 'success') with them." (Benefit statement, statement of success/commercial.)

"Is this an area you are involved in?" or "May I ask how involved you are in . . . ?" or "To what extent are you involved in/interested in/is this a priority/an area of interest for you . . . ?" (Need question—get okay.)

"Great. Do you have a *few* minutes?" or "Is this a good time to talk for a *few* minutes?" (Time check—rapport.)

"First, to make sure I am focusing on . . . , may I ask . . . ?" (Qualify, identify needs—optional.)

"I'd like to meet with you to . . . " or "I'll
be in Philadelphia on . . . see some of my
good clients such as . . . When would be a
good time next week to get together?" or
"I'll be in on Tuesday and Wednesday.
Would it make sense to get together
briefly to . . . ?"

(Ask for the appoint-
ment, make second ef-
fort, or confirm.)

In analyzing this exchange, notice that your need/benefit statement is key to the process, since you are on the telephone and are
subject to all the drawbacks (and advantages) of the telephone.
Because it is the phone, your customers can disengage very easily.
Comments like, "Sorry, I'm busy," or "Don't call me, I'm not interested," can result in a disconnect. In a face-to-face call, there is
more time; you are in the office. But on the phone there is less
time to capture the interest of your prospect. So you must be *fast*
but *not slick*. These special aspects of telephone selling have led
many salespeople to make exaggerated claims or ask leading
questions like, "Do you want to save money?" Today's sophisticated and cynical prospects will not be impressed by those tactics.
The phone, also by its nature, can depersonalize. There is no
handshake, no eye contact by which to meet face-to-face and be
humanized with one another. But, unfortunately, many attempts
at rapport on a "cold" prospect call are read by the prospect as
ingenuine. So, unless the area of the country or prospect you are
calling seems to allow for more chitchat or offers more leeway in
being friendly and casual, reserve the rapport for later and limit
it to a friendly voice, an efficient manner, and an indication there
is something in it for the *prospect*. To help strengthen your need
and benefit statement, *bolster* it with proof. You can do this in two
ways: First, mention some prestigious clients, *and*, second, mention your successes with them. The prospect will think, "Well, if
that company works with them, they can't be all that bad." Once
you have played your ace—presented your need/benefit statement—check for the level of prospect interest. Many successful
top prospectors ask if the area or benefit they mentioned is one
the person is involved or interested in. If the need/benefit statement and name dropping has taken hold, they get a yes. To make
sure you communicate that you have a customer focus, one more

check is in order: Ask if the prospect has time to talk for a *few* minutes, underscoring the word few. The sensible and relevant need/benefit statement and the checking help separate you from pesky intruders.

Once you have an okay, depending on your need to qualify and what you perceive to be the prospect's tolerance for questions, ask a few qualifying questions to make sure you do not drive, for example, 150 miles when the prospect has an interest *but* no budget or need. You may also need to position information about your product. The key is not to go too far in telling or qualifying or you may talk yourself out of the appointment. Depending on your prospect list, geographical area, cost of sale, and so on, you can determine how much qualifying you need to do. Up to this point, this prospect is likely to be a *suspect,* and some qualifying is usually needed. Just because prospects are interested does *not* mean they are qualified. It is also important not to spend too much time qualifying. Consider what happened to one printer when an association executive called to make an appointment to discuss printing a prestigious and high-run newsletter. The "salesperson" who answered the telephone asked so many technical questions (number of pages, frequency, screens, and so on), that the executive, interested in the big picture, not the nitty-gritty, gave up. Fortunately, his editorial consultant knew the printer gave excellent service and alerted the president of the printing company to call the executive to make amends – and make the sale! Of course, if your universe of prospects is very large and dispersed or if the cost of the sales call is significant in terms of time and dollars and qualifying is important, ask for anything from needs to budget information. One top-producing computer salesperson says she will *not* go out to see a prospect until she knows three things: time frames for making a decision, decision-making process, and *budget.* Her reasons are that in her industry, many customers are "tire kickers," curious or looking for no-cost consulting. But telephone qualifying is usually at best semiqualifying. Once you have qualified the prospect, avoid getting into the specifics that you want to cover in the sales call. Phone qualifying is more like quasi-qualifying with the real qualifying taking place at the call.

The process of qualifying serves two purposes. It helps you identify hot, warm, back-burner, and no-opportunity situations.

One insurance salesperson says he can identify China eggs, accounts that will never hatch, over the phone by asking a few questions. Qualifying also helps you identify needs and maximize your time. Once you are satisfied that the prospect qualifies, set the appointment: time, place, and people.

Of course, in spite of your professional approach, prospects will say no. And since this no can be as much a knee-jerk reaction as an indication of disinterest, be prepared to give a second effort by using the objection resolution model:

■ Show *empathy:* "Yes, I can understand."

■ *Ask why:* "May I ask why that isn't a concern for you, since . . . ?" or "May I ask why you are not interested?" This can often give you an opening. Either with reshaping of your objective you can find an opportunity, or, if your original premise is off, you can find a different in.

■ Position your benefit and perhaps add or change the benefit, depending on the prospect's response.

■ Restate your request for the appointment and add on a *20- to 30-minute time limit* for the call.

The above approach (the objection resolution model) will help you avoid making a product dump or pushing hard. As you make your second effort, *put a time limit on the appointment,* and this often will get you in. Of course, be sure to honor that time promise when you are with the prospect.

What should you do if the prospect says no after you give a second effort and have used the 20-minute tactic? Depending on the strength of the no, you probably should accept the no—for then anyway. Your judgment is key here, but at some point you will need to say thank you and leave the door open with a comment like, "Thank you for your time. I'd like to try you back in . . . Thank you." If customers say they are in a time crunch, ask when you can call back and follow up as agreed. If the customer says, "We just bought X . . . ," at least get competitive information: "How is it going?" "When . . . ?" Then call in a few weeks to find out if indeed it is going at all! You may find an opportunity waiting for you!

Salespeople make a few common mistakes when they face telephone prospect objections. Let's consider—and avoid—these gaffes:

- Salespeople give up—they simply quit. A prospect says, "I'm not interested," and they say okay and hang up. They are calling, not selling. Preparation, confidence, empathy, question, second effort—prospecting requires relentless effort.

- Sometimes salespeople give up less directly, jumping to the future and accepting first rejection by asking when they should call back. For example, the prospect may say, "I just bought one," and these salespeople say, "Well, when will you be looking at another one?... Okay, next year," instead of saying something like, "Oh, I understand. May I ask what you bought? How is it going?...," to get a sense of what needs were met and which remain.

- Some salespeople contradict the prospect, rudely—"No you don't"—or politely, "But we have a better . . . "

- Salespeople sometimes simply *ignore* the prospect comment— "Well, can I just tell you about a few of our new products?"— *and proceed to make a product dump.* The better their products are, the more likely they are to do this!

- Some salespeople masquerade as consultative: They use the "empathy *but*": "I am happy to hear you are satisfied but . . . ," and the *but* ushers in the contradiction, or they ask a question, but the *wrong* question! They use self-serving, leading, insulting questions like, "Don't you want to increase productivity?", not a question to get at the heart of the objection.

Instead of the buts, the quitting, the defensiveness, use the consultative approach by showing empathy, asking a question, positioning your response, and checking. The alternatives to this are to give up or become defensive!

Many salespeople describe getting the appointment as the greatest challenge. Getting through barriers, from screeners to prospects who object for themselves, is difficult. Prospects are trying to protect their time and their pocketbooks. They *are* testing the caller to figure out if the call is worthwhile. Know-how and persistence are required, as are staying hungry and remaining confident. The rewards are tremendous.

Referrals

Now let's look at some tactics you can use to warm up a cold call and get through gatekeepers. The best way to get an appointment with a prospect is to turn a "cold call" to someone you don't know into a "warm call" by having a hinge, or referral, or connection which will help pave the way and open the door for you. Having a referral or having another strong hinge like an association connection is the best way to increase your odds for success. One of the best tactics you can use in identifying and reaching new prospects is to get *referrals* from present, satisfied customers. *The key is to ask your present, satisfied customers for referrals.* For example, "John, since you are satisfied with . . . , I was wondering if you would have the names of a few colleagues I might contact who might benefit. . . . " Once customers give you a name, send letters to the customers thanking them for their referrals. You can also send letters expressly designed to ask customers for the names of their colleagues. Then follow up with a telephone call. Once you get a name, find out as much as possible to get insights into the person, and, when possible, ask your contact to pave the way for you with a personal introduction, telephone call, or letter. Don't forget an excellent time to ask for a referral is right after you have done a good job or a "favor."

Referrals are very helpful because they can warm up that first call. They increase your credibility and make the prospect more receptive to you. *Peer-to-peer referrals* can be very powerful. One computer salesperson is an expert at this. He finds out which organizations his prospects belong to and then he tries to identify one of his present customers who belongs to that organization. He then asks this customer to call prospects to say how satisfied they are with his system and to suggest that it might be a good idea for them to speak with the salesperson. Many customers say they appreciate this kind of peer-to-peer referral as a way to help them sort out who to see. Top salespeople realize that "Everybody knows somebody." Find that "everybody" and ask him or her to make the introduction and help pave the way to "somebody"!

A referral is a type of hinge, a connection with the customer to make the contact less cold. Other hinges are:

- Business hinge: "I am a colleague of . . . ; I'm calling . . . "

- Leverage of a social contact: "Tom Smith said he saw you in New York. . . . How did you enjoy the show?" or (at the museum gala) "Bob, I'd like to get together about . . . , I'll ring you next week. . . . " (Keep it short; don't be a bore.)

- Follow-up on mailings, industry or product information: "Tom (or Mr. X), we sent you a letter about . . . Have you . . . ?" When you are having difficulty reaching a customer by telephone, you can use a letter to help pave the way for your telephone call. One salesperson uses the strategy of writing to the president of a company and ends his letter saying he will call the president's secretary to find out whom to call about X. In this way, he gets directed to the right person and then leverages the referral from the president's office — many seniors like this approach. Be sure if you send letters that you do so in manageable waves so you can handle the telephone follow-up.

- Summary of last contact: "Mary, about X, I said I'd get back to you. I've spoken to our . . . They say . . . "

- Track record: "We've done . . . " You can share accomplishments of your organization, such as ratings, listenings, performance.

- Market information: sharing market color (information about what is happening in the market, on the Street, in the customer's industry; a window of opportunity that has opened or is closing; overall industry news, trends, research; your specialists' or economists' reading of the market; or any other information that would affect or interest the customer or company).

- Homework, research: for example, a clipping from the newspaper — "I read in . . . and thought . . . "

- Event or customer seminar: "We are having . . . would like to invite you and . . . "

- *Anything new:* "We have just merged. . . . " *Anything new such as a new product or new person creates an excellent reason to call customers/prospects.*

- Target group campaign: "We are contacting members of X Association to . . . We are offering . . . "

- Current situation or observed prospect need: (Broker) "Mary, because of X Company's recent . . . to discuss with you . . . how we could (benefit) . . . "

Having a referral, however, is the ultimate hinge, since it helps build your credibility. Of course, the other hinges or linkages can also be effective. By referring to any person, event, organization, or activity that you share with the prospective client, you can establish a *common ground.* Don't think you can't find a connection. By doing homework, you can usually find something that you share with the prospect, such as school ties, events such as a trade show you both attended, professional associations, or a sporting club you both enjoy. Keep in mind, "Everybody knows somebody." You can also refer to any articles you may have seen about the client company. At the very least, you may be able to refer to a letter you sent in advance of your call.

Have Positive References Ready

Also, as you prepare to make your prospect call, have references handy. References can help you build credibility with prospects who don't know you. By referring to prestigious customers in general, you can often interest prospects in talking to you. Do so in a tactful, not a name-dropping or boastful, way. Remember, however, before you offer specific names of customers as references, to get permission from the individual first. Make certain, *before* you give a name as a reference, you know what kind of reference you will get! Almost nothing can be as damaging as a bad reference, especially at a peer-to-peer level. The best way to make sure of the kind of reference you will get is to begin by calling customers and asking them if you can use them as references. This is not only good manners, but it is smart. First, calling gives you a chance to rekindle good feelings. Second, calling gives you a chance to find out where the customer stands. If you don't know, before you mention the reference, tactfully ask, "How is X going?" If there are problems, fix them and find another reference. Calling the client in advance also gives you a chance to highlight what your prospect is interested in hearing. The bottom line is that this courteous gesture usually makes the reference more willing to talk and talk positively. Once your client has served as your reference, thank the client. Don't forget to call your prospect to check if he or she was able to get through to the references and then use the call to find out how things stand. Say, "I know some people are difficult to reach. Have you been able to talk to . . . ?" "How satisfied . . . ? Any concerns . . . ?" "Any questions?"

Develop a list of references you can count on. Keep checking the list. Don't abuse references' willingness to speak to prospects; alternate. Send your customers who serve as references thank you notes, entertain them, and remember them at holiday time. One smart salesperson called a customer who complained frequently (but when the salesperson attempted to change anything, the customer blocked it) to ask directly what kind of reference he would give. The customer said, "I think you are great, but I'd say for X, Y, and Z I'd use (a competitor)." After the salesperson asked why and then thanked him for his feedback, the customer was quickly eliminated from the reference list.

What to Do about a Bad Reference

Even if you check out all your references, you may find that you get a bad or less than sterling reference. By checking with prospects about how the references are going, you hopefully will be able to identify the negative reference before it is too late. When a prospect gets a negative reference and tells you about it, first of all, be appreciative. Don't become defensive with your prospect.

Ask questions to get *specific* details. Then if you need time, say you would like to look into it. Once you have your data, develop and then present your information to offset the negative press. The key is to get *details* from the prospect and then take corrective measures. For example, a salesperson tells how a prospect called him and said, "I hear you lost X account." This was news to the salesperson and, instead of becoming defensive, she said, "Well, you may know more than I do about this. To my knowledge, we have an excellent relationship with them. For example, in September . . . but may I ask what you heard?" The prospect explained what he heard—from an unidentified source (that turned out to be a competitor!)—about the problem, an installation that had gone awry in Chicago. The story had a grain of truth to it. The salesperson explained the full situation and then gave the customer the name of two other customers in the same organization, one a salesperson and one a manager in a regional office. From ongoing experience with these customers, the salesperson knew that they were very satisfied with her organization. She also knew the source of the complaint in the customer organization. The source of the complaint was a manager who dropped the ball. The salesperson called two more senior customers first, to explain the situation and ask them to accept the call from the prospect. They were more than willing to say their company was responsible for the *small* glitch and that they were very pleased with the entire relationship. After talking with them, the prospect was satisfied. He became upset by the *misrepresentation* by a competitor. The deal moved forward.

If you get a bad reference, it may be useful, if it is possible, to suggest that your prospect speak with a more senior customer in the same organization. If there were a snag, a senior will give a fuller, more accurate picture, especially if he or she was involved in the decision to use your services. But check this out first. Often seniors are less critical and are more willing to share in some of the blame for problems. If no senior can be identified, urge your prospect to get at least a "second opinion" from another customer in the organization.

Letters

When you don't have a personal reference, you can use a letter to warm up what otherwise would be a cold telephone call. A letter can be an effective way to connect with the customer, and it gives you a point of reference to use with secretaries or gatekeepers: "I'm calling in reference to my letter to *X*." Conclude your letter with a thank you and a time *you* will be calling. End your letters with an action step that *you* will take, and be sure to follow up as promised. Many excellent prospectors prefer to speak to the prospect briefly, get a lay of the land so they can tailor the letter or package they will send. Then they follow up the letter with another telephone call.

Skills for Getting Past Secretaries/Gatekeepers

Often the first challenge is to get through gatekeepers and secretaries. Some tactics you can use with them are:

- Treat secretaries with respect. Be friendly and cheerful—not condescending or sugary.
- If you can't get through, take responsibility for following up. You may leave your number, but don't wait for the prospect to return your call.
- Personalize the conversation by *getting* and using the gatekeeper's or secretary's name. Be sure to put the secretary's name on your rolodex in your customer profile.
- When appropriate, remember holidays and birthdays with gifts such as chocolates, flowers, tickets to a show.
- Be appreciative. Say that you appreciate them and compliment them to their managers.
- Send and refer to a letter.
- Ask for the help of the secretary: "Can you help me and give me an idea what would be the best time to call?" or "When would be a good time to call?" Ask questions to find out exactly

when the prospect will be in. Ask, "Does she get in by 8:00?" The secretary often will give you information. He or she may say, "Well, he's usually here by 7:30."

- If you find you must send materials, say to the secretary, "May I send these to you? I know X gets so much mail. Would you see it gets on his desk?" Then include a personal note thanking the secretary. When you call the secretary, you may now have a stake in helping you get through.

- In general terms, give your purpose for calling, if asked. Don't insinuate that your topic is too important or too complex for the "mere" secretary to understand. Give a reason secretaries are less likely to question: "I'm with X. I am calling about personal banking matters."

- When giving your reason for calling, be prepared with a possible, *tailored* benefit: "I have a product or service that I think X will be very interested in."

- Give only your name—secretaries usually will ask one qualifying question. Let that question be about who you are with.

- Call around the secretary's hours, when a customer is likely to answer his or her own telephone (call before 8:30 a.m. or after 5:30 p.m.).

- Call mid-Friday afternoon in the summer, when customers are likely to be in their offices hoping to "cut out early." Taking your call can help justify their being there!

Disciplined Prospecting System

Prospecting requires discipline. It demands preparation. But not the kind of preparation one young salesman was doing. His colleague jokingly asked, "Hey, Bob, why aren't you on the phone?" Bob, perusing an annual report, replied, "I'm getting ready for a business development call." The problem was it was 11:00 a.m., prime time when Bob should have been calling, *not* preparing. Now let's look at an approach to determine how many calls to make and how to make them:

- First, figure out what an "acceptable" number of prospect telephone calls per day or per week are by using this formula to analyze the revenues and numbers to determine the amount of prospecting you have to do to meet your annual sales objectives.

Your annual sales objective	$_____
Existing customers (how much are you counting on from present customers?)	$_____
New customers (annual sales objectives minus $ from existing customers)	$_____
Average size of deal	$_____
Number of new customers based on average size of deal	_____
Number of qualified prospects to gain one new customer	_____
Number of prospects to contact to get one qualified prospect	_____
Prospecting plan	
Number of prospect phone calls per year:	_____
per month:	_____
per week:	_____

- Save a *block* of time to make calls—don't squeeze them or do one here and one there between other things
- Schedule preparation time that is *not* during prime time.
- Make a priority list of names to call and an objective for each call—with notations on the best time to call.
- Set up a system for taking and organizing notes from the phone calls.
- Use a follow-up tickler system for tracking results, call-backs.

- Establish an "acceptable" number of times you will ask for and get referrals from satisfied customers.

Persistence

Just a few words on persistence, since it is very important. In all sales, objections come with the territory. It is a major part of the territory in telephone selling. Telephone selling depersonalizes. It is easier to dodge calls, disengage, be rude, say no, and so on. To maintain your motivation, it is key to understand and respect the concept of a "hit ratio" and not become discouraged by "not interested." You will not sell with every deal or every prospect. A senior in a top firm wisely remarked, "You don't *earn* every sale you get, and you don't get every sale you earn." With this in mind, develop *resiliency* and persistence. Sometimes you will be on a roll, and sometimes you will feel as if you have run into a brick wall.

Because of the nature of telephone contact, it can be difficult to reach customers or prospects. And a wave of "nos" can be discouraging. Persistence, know-how, and follow-up are the essence of what it takes to be successful in getting appointments with prospects. Almost no sales effort requires as much persistence as telephone prospecting. Telephone selling is not for the faint of heart. Some salespeople new to telephone selling are even concerned about being "too" persistent. They often express this concern as "not wanting to bother the customer"; they say that "if my customers need something, they call me." As mentioned earlier, these attitudes are often related to a misunderstanding of what selling is all about coupled with a fear of rejection. Although the concern about not wanting to pester people is legitimate, it can be an easy out, a way of rationalizing not making that first or tenth telephone call or avoiding those follow-up calls. And the first call at worst, if handled professionally, is an interruption not an intrusion.

Some salespeople confuse persistence with hard sell, but persistence is not synonymous with hard selling. Hard selling is, at its best, product selling and, at its worst, manipulation. Think of the salesperson who asks, "Don't you want to save money?" early in the phone call. He or she is using a leading question to manipulate. What can the customer say, this salesperson asks. But today's sophisticated customer won't fall for this manipulative tactic and will probably react negatively, feeling insulted. Neither hard selling nor product selling are effective today, because customers are too knowledgeable. They have, as the expression goes, "been around the block."

The good news is you can be persistent and consultative at the same time. How? Keep in mind that you want to *help* the customer. If you succeed in helping the customer, you help yourself and your organization—it's a *win-win*. When you help the customer, you share in the customer's success. If you think you have something of value for the customer, state it succinctly and then check how interested the customer is. High-pressure selling, far from helping the customer, badgers, cajoles, and manipulates the customer. Hard sell isn't effective in an environment of sophisticated customers and heavy competition. But neither is what is called "soft selling." The problem with "soft sell" is that it is too often akin to apathy. Soft selling usually means being available but not being proactive. A soft-sell salesperson might say, "Customers know what they want. I tell them about X and they make up their minds," or, "I wanted you to know about X. Let me know if you have an interest," or, "I'm selling X." (Customer says, "I'm not interested") and the salesperson says, "Okay, thank you. . . . " These approaches are a disservice to everybody—the customer, the sales organization, and the salesperson. These approaches are calling, order taking, not selling. The salesperson, hopefully, knows the product better than the customer. It is the salesperson's *responsibility* to understand customer's needs and position the product as a solution to needs. Of course this means you must prepare for prospect calls—yes, prepare. Another kind of selling recently in vogue has been dubbed "sentimental selling." This is a friendly, down-home, no-pressure type selling that is typified in the Bartle & Jaymes commercials where salespeople (friends) give home-spun advice. But do you see them asking and answering questions? Consultative selling is neither hard, soft, nor sentimental selling. It is *need-based selling,* and it requires a disciplined approach of questioning and listening. Finally, consultative selling requires being proactive — initiating opportunities and facing the rejection which comes with proactive sales.

It is impossible to be successful in a competitive marketplace if you can't cope with rejection. Most top performers don't like rejection any more than the next person, but *salespeople who are persistent* are willing to call, call back, and think of creative ways to reach their prospects. But their persistence is not just raw aggression. Instead, they believe that what they have is of value to the customer — quite the opposite of "bothering" the customer. And while they don't enjoy a wave of nos, they don't let them sink in — or sink them. They spring back and keep going.

An example of persistence is the top salesperson who got the name of a prospect from a good present customer who knew his friend was opening outlet 14. There was one catch. She didn't have his number, and the new store didn't have a telephone or a sign. But the salesperson finally got to the prospect, a man noted for his Midas touch. The prospect said, "If you could find me before we opened here, I want you for my banker!"

Persistence gets *measurable* results. When 25 *top-performing* sales and trading generalists were asked, "Once you met a prospect, when would you telephone him?" Without exception each person polled said, "The next day at the latest." When asked what they would do if the prospect did not call them back and it was 2:00 p.m., one half would call no later than 8:30 a.m. the next morning, and the other half said, "Call immediately."

Most prospects are already involved with a supplier from their banker to the company who supplies water for their water cooler. Their common objections are "I already have one," "I am concerned," "I'm satisfied," "We just signed a contract," and so on. It takes persistence to get through these barriers. In some businesses, it takes as much as a 2-year effort or more to land an account. Therefore, successful telephone salespeople need to be persistent and resourceful. One salesperson landed her largest account thanks to top-notch creativity. She learned that the managing director of a major New York investment bank was the decision maker in choosing a vendor to provide technical training for the Chicago office. She tried unsuccessfully for several months to reach him, but he was forever "not available" for her telephone calls, and he never returned them. On a trip to Chicago she decided to try to see him. When she called the switchboard at 8:00 a.m., there was no answer. She thought that perhaps by calling 01 instead of the 00 digit at the end of the telephone number, she might be able to reach him, since seniors often get the first line. The managing director answered his own telephone. After introducing herself, her firm, and stating that she had tried to reach him to discuss the training, she invited him to lunch. He responded by saying, "You have a nerve calling me on my private line. I won't even bother to ask how you got this number. I am a very busy man. For your information, it takes at least 3 weeks to get on my calendar. How dare you call me!" She said, "I don't mean to offend you. I have been trying *for months* to reach you, I know we have . . . that I think would (benefit)," then she *repeated,* "Would you like to have lunch today?" He said, "Well, (pause) yes, be here at 11:55, and I need to be finished with lunch at 12:55. I'm on the third floor at . . . Can you remember that?" She had already qualified this prospect. Her goal was clear and simple (not easy) — to get an appointment. The salesperson was resourceful. She didn't take no for an answer. Once she got in, her skills and product did the rest. This customer became one of her largest accounts.

There is also the well-known story of how a salesperson got a major account back — one that made his career. He sold advertising space for a major magazine based in New York. One prospect on his target list was a *Fortune* 100 company located in Atlanta that years before had canceled its advertising contract with his magazine because of explicit photographs that the customer found objectionable. The account was generally considered a "lost cause." After 3 months of telephone calls, *the salesperson finally got through to his potential buyer at lunchtime when the customer picked up his own telephone.* As he expected, the customer reiterated the company's position not to advertise in his magazine and refused to set an appointment. But the salesperson was persistent and innovative. He revealed that he was from Atlanta and that he would like to get home to visit his mother. He asked for a 15-minute appointment and pointed out he could tie it to a trip home. He took a calculated risk, but what did he really have to lose? What he said was true. In fact, his regional ties were a factor in the decision of the magazine to hire him for the territory. The customer softened and agreed to a 10-minute appointment. When the salesperson arrived at the customer's office, he presented him with a jar of home-made peach preserves, compliments of his mother. By the end of the meeting, the salesperson had sold a small ad.

The point is that persistence and resourcefulness go hand in hand, along with the conviction that you have something of value for the customer based on a belief in your product and your homework. All these qualities are important in telephone selling whether you are calling a prospect who is predisposed to like you, has an ax to grind from a previous negative experience, or has no ax to grind but no interest either. Telephone selling to prospects is truly character building. It is, as one successful telephone salesperson described it, "the forging of steel!"

Usually there is less resistance when selling to present customers, but persistence and creativity are also needed with present relationships. Certainly the fact that your present customers are your competitors' prospects should be enough to spur attention. Unfortunately, some good customers are treated like an old shoe. Although there is no set formula for how often to call and what to talk about, there are guidelines based on factors such as the nature of your sale, your industry standards, and the profitability of the relationship. With ongoing relationships, if you are talking to your customers less than once a month you are probably missing business and relationship opportunities. One way to check about your frequency of calling is to ask your customers directly. This will give you your answer situation by situation. Contact can range from several times a day to one time per quarter depending on the customer, relationship, product, market, and so on. For example, a stockbroker or an institutional salesperson may call a customer ten times a day depending on the situation, certainly at a minimum of one time a week.

How much information to give and get in one call varies according to the salesperson's style and the customer's needs. Some salespeople like to make a "power call" filled with four or five reasons they are calling. Others isolate subjects so they have reasons to keep calling. Certainly this is the best approach if keeping contact is an issue.

As far as what to talk about, the answer to this question is like the answer to the question, "Where can a gorilla sit?" The answer, of course, is "Wherever it wants to." What can you talk to a customer about? *Whatever the customer is interested in.* It is up to *you* to find out what interests your customers—market color, a new idea, an idea that was tested and worked, industry update, specific ideas, tidbits of information, product benefits, the Mets game, sailing, best wishes for a holiday, and so on. Your role is to find out what interests your customers and talk about it.

Persistence is a state of mind beginning with the concept that you have something of value to offer. Persistence is behavioral—making those calls and selling. Persistence means sending a card or letter, calling, and finding creative ways and new reasons to keep those cards, letters, and *calls* coming.

Summary

Many salespeople consider prospecting "the forging of steel." If you can succeed at *it*, you can sell. As challenging as prospecting is and as fraught as it is with rejection, prospecting keeps the pipeline full. It gives you a chance to stay fresh. It can also help you stay humble, not in a negative way but to keep you in touch with the market, with the customer. Each time you succeed in getting an appointment with a good prospect, recognize that as a point for celebration. It is an accomplishment, and it is a beginning. For all the nos you are apt to run into, keep your chin up, learn from them. Learn something about your prospect, learn something about your product, learn something about yourself. Pick up the phone and start a relationship.

PART 5
Special Situations

19
Special
Telephone
Situations

Telephone Conference Calls

Team selling is a fact of life today. As selling situations have become increasingly complex and competitive, team calls can increase client comfort and expertise. Group selling can occur face-to-face or by telephone in the form of conference calls. Conference calling doesn't replace face-to-face calls; it can build on them. If you aren't using conference calling, you may miss multiple opportunities to service your clients. Conference call advantages enable you to respond promptly to client needs and to leverage resources. Whether you need to marshall seniors, specialists, colleagues, or your assistant, the conference call enables you to bring any of or all these additional resources to the client in a cost-effective and time-efficient way.

Many salespeople don't like conference calls. They feel such calls *further* reduce the level of personal contact or intimacy of one-on-one telephone selling. Such salespeople also worry about being able to control the situation. One recruiter described being on a conference call to feeling like "a bowl of fruit in the middle of the table with everybody grabbing!" Obviously with several players, possibly on both sides, one needs to orchestrate parties. This takes both preparation and know-how. Let's look at how to manage conference calls to maximize the benefits and contain the risks.

Control begins with being prepared. Even though conference calls cost less in time and money than team face-to-face calls, they require every bit as much preparation. Whether you are calling alone or with team members, it is essential to know what your objectives are. When team members are involved it is doubly—even triply—necessary that your objectives be clear and shared.

When team members will be involved, clarify roles early—decide who will do what and why *before* the call. One bank was masterful in how it organized and implemented its conference call strategy. The bank's top objective was to expand key accounts by cross-selling a new product into prequalified priority relationships. Their strategy involved leveraging existing relationships introducing a product specialist. First, the generalists would send clients letters (hinge or referral) introducing the specialists and the product concepts. Each letter ended with an action step in which the generalist requested the opportunity to telephone the client to introduce the specialist. The objective of the telephone call was to have the specialist arrange a time to meet with the client, *without* the generalist. This strategy was well conceived and orchestrated, and it worked!

But conference calling can be tricky if you are not ready for it. It has its own set of business etiquette and its own built-in traps. Some guidelines to help you control the situation and maintain rapport:

- Plan the call with your teammates so that your team knows and agrees on the objective of the telephone call and all players understand the strategy, objectives, and their roles.

- Make sure you know who will be on the client's team and their roles.

- Keep on top of your time. In conference calls, as in any group sales presentations, being on time and knowing how much time you have can be far more critical than in one-on-one situations. It is difficult enough to recover from missing or being late for a telephone call with one client, but to be "missing in action" when four clients are gathered, waiting (impatiently) in a room or in various offices is even worse. Mistakes like this in a "public" forum are not forgotten easily, if ever.

- Under most circumstances arrange the conference call with the client ahead of time and determine the amount of time you will need for the call.

- Whenever possible, sit in the same room with your teammates so that you can maintain eye contact and communicate with each other through signals and notes.

- Introduce each teammate by name, function, purpose of his or her participation in the call. Identify all players on your team.

- After you check with your team members to make sure they are ready, call your client and say, "John, I will be putting Tom Barber and . . . on the line with us to . . . OK?" If for some reason, this is impossible or unnecessary (client is expecting the call from your team), immediately tell the party you are calling that you have X and Y on the line with you so that the client does not say something that he or she would *not* have said with a third party on the line. This is *one* rare time when interrupting a client could be appropriate. Just jump in and say, "John, I'd like to let you know I have X on the line."

- Once you introduce your team, if the client does not reciprocate introductions, *ask who is there*. Then be sure to say hello — and at the end, goodbye — to each person.

- Once you know who is present, make certain you know each person's role. When you do not know the role of each person, *ask*, "To get a better understanding of the kind of information you may need, may I ask Sandra's role?" or " . . . where Sandra fits in?"

- Use the six critical skills, especially relating (*never* embarrass someone in the presence of others), questioning, and listening. Do not interrupt! Be patient.

- Take notes, attributing remarks and needs to specific clients.

- Check. If one client has a question, check after you answered it to find out if your response has satisfied the client. Then remember to ask if there are any other questions.

- Include all clients, as appropriate. If, for example, Bill gives his view, ask, "Thank you, Bill. John, do you have any points to add? What about you, Mary?"

- Involve all parties in the discussion. In addition to including everybody in greeting and goodbye, take advantage of opportunities to mention parties who have been quiet during the call. Say, as you are concluding, "When you and X (quiet person) receive . . . ," or "Fine, I'll call you on Tuesday and if you or X have any questions before then. . . . "

- Take notes and keep track of who is saying what.

- Use the hold button if you need a few minutes to regroup.

- If people in the meeting have been helpful (you're working with them on the topic under discussion), be sure to comment on and thank them publicly (unless of course they were your personal "coach," helping you on the side).

- Follow up with a letter when appropriate to summarize decisions, next step, and/or key points of the discussion.

Whether you are making the call solo or with your team, if you are selling to several clients via the telephone conference call, keep in mind that it is more difficult for clients to follow your ideas and materials when you are not there in person. There are some tips for using materials during telephone conference calls (or one-on-one telephone calls):

- Send materials in advance whenever possible — one full set for each client who will be involved. In advance ask how many sets the client will need.

- Number each page and/or use tabs and headings for easy reference.

- At the beginning of the call check if the clients have the materials with them.

- Create an agenda and use it. After the opening, quickly walk through the entire agenda (about five or six key points at most normally) and then check if the agenda items meet the client's expectations.

- Introduce each discussion with where you are. For example,

"Kate, Jeff, J.J.—if you will look at the grey folder, page 6 covers . . . Any questions? . . . Now please turn to . . . " This is especially true if your client group is mixed, for example, if two clients are on the speaker telephone while you are presenting face-to-face to the other clients.

- If you are showing an exhibit that the client does not have, begin by saying, "Beth and Mac, I'm going to show . . . Since you do not have a copy of this document, I'll talk you through the ideas. . . . "
- Fax whatever materials you can to clients who did not receive the materials earlier, during the meeting, if necessary.

Squawk Box

Many people don't like being put on the speaker telephone or "squawk box." The reception quality is generally inferior, and they feel "exposed." Also, the question of trust on all sides can come up, since one party may not divulge who is present. A squawk box can be used as a power tool to indirectly say, "I'm important. . . . " When you are on or use a squawk box, take control. Ask who is there, since most clients will divulge players if asked. You might say, "Bill, will anyone else be joining us?" or "Who else is there so I can address any concerns they may have?" Usually the more often you are involved with a squawk box, the more comfortable you become.

Fax

Fax it! These two little words make communication via the facsimile sound so easy, and it is. The use of the fax as a way to communicate with clients is exploding as salespeople discover the speed and convenience of this relatively new technology. Yet in spite of all its advantages, the fax contains several potential traps for the salesperson.

Complacency ranks as the number-one trap. The fax technology that once offered a unique advantage is now commonplace across the board and across continents. So the challenge of using the fax in sales situations now parallels the challenge of face-to-face and telephone selling in the nineties: how to differentiate and gain a competitive edge.

Fax fever poses another trap. Many salespeople fax things that don't need to be faxed. One client complained bitterly that he received a time-sensitive document too late because it was faxed. The salesperson located *across the street* was so accustomed to faxing materials that he faxed the client a 150-page document! He forgot that faxing takes time. Another salesperson faxed a letter although he knew the client would be away for a week. A mailed letter—crisp and easier to read—would have been more appropriate.

Passivity poses yet another problem. As a salesperson, in sending a fax, think about why you are doing it—to get business. One very successful broker says she never sends a "passive" fax. She avoids faxing materials a client can look at and feel "finished" with. Instead, she sends materials that require client interpretation. For example, rather than sending data in a list, she sends it in graph form, knowing the client is likely to want her interpretation. Then she calls to discuss.

Telling all on a fax is yet another mistake. One salesperson cautions against putting all his "aces" on the faxes he sends his clients. "Why would you do that? Then you are dead," he says.

Certainly revealing price in a fax can be a mistake. Remember how close the CEO of the "fax wars" story came to losing one of his oldest clients? A price is just a number on a page, but value is relative. Putting price on a fax can make it easier for clients to create "bid" situations by asking several competitors to submit a price.

If your client faxes the request for a price to you, and you think a bid situation is being created, call the client, discuss the request, and ask to see the client (if it is important and feasible). Be persuasive. If it is a competitive situation, you need to find a way to differentiate your offer other than price.

Be sensitive to the quality of the fax. One salesperson who has excellent relationships with his customer's secretaries asks them to make copies of what he faxes if the fax is not produced on individual sheets or if the receiving fax uses flimsy "thermo" paper. Another salesperson had the same thought. He sent his client a copy of an article that the client wanted to send to trainees in her company. The considerate salesperson followed up to ask if the client needed an original for copying purposes. Her answer: "No, but thanks. It copied great." Think about appearance and convenience of reading the fax. Despite the move to normal paper, some clients still use thermo paper or do not have individual sheets.

Differentiating Your Fax

- Remember, the use of the fax is exploding, so don't flood your client with your faxes.

- When you use the fax, have a clear objective in mind.

- Formalize your cover page. Explain what is being faxed. Personalize it. Say thank you. Mention your action step.

- For important documents, call the client or client's secretary to check if the fax got through.

- Do not count on your administrative staff to recognize they are faxing two-sided pages. Either make a clear notation that the document contains double-sided pages or make copies of side 2.

- If appearance is a factor, follow up your fax with a hard copy or use overnight mail.

Preparing the Fax

The fax can be an alternative type of sales call providing information, service, and momentum to the sale. Just as with a sales call consider:

Objective: What is your reason for sending the fax?
- Is it measurable?

- Is there a time frame?

Customer Needs: How does your objective relate to a customer's needs?
- Have you included *benefits* as well as features?

Objections: What objections do you anticipate?
- How do you plan to respond to these objections? How can you offset them?

  Empathy
  Questions

Action Step: Keep in mind why you are using the fax—to get something done. So build in an action step.
- What action step have you planned?
- What action step do you want the client to use?

Voice Mail

Voice mail has spread throughout corporate America. When you make a phone call, get ready to go "on stage." Be prepared to leave a voice mail or answering machine message. Keep it clear, short, and accurate. One client complained of not only having too many messages from salespeople — as many as 20 a day! — but finding messages that were long and boring. It is very annoying for the listener to have to wade through a slow and confused message. Pick up the pace but slow down when you state your telephone number. Point out a potential *benefit,* and if you'd like leave your name and number, but don't count on having your call returned. The real key is to leave the door open for you to call back: "Since I will be out . . . " It also helps to tell the people you are calling that you would appreciate a few minutes of their time. By limiting the time commitment you are more likely to get through later. Although a sense of good manners might make you feel obliged to leave a message, please remember you are hearing and dealing with an electronic voice, not the individual, so feel free to hang up and not leave a message. Before doing this, however, consider whether your client has caller ID. For example, if you were to call an investment bank via a highly sensitive area like M&A, the number from which you called would be recorded, and, if the company knows you in its memory, your name would also appear. It is useful to let your prospect/client know you called: leave your name/company/phone number and the purpose of your call. Say that you will call back.

There are ways to get around voice mail if you suspect that the number you are reaching is one reserved for unsolicited sales/prospect calls. To find an alternative route to the prospect, call the company's central number to reach the operator. Ask him or her if there is another number or get the phone number of your prospect's secretary. If you don't have success with either of these tactics, find someone else you might speak with. Go up or down the ladder to a person more senior or junior.

If your have a voice mail, make sure your message is professional and brief. You can take advantage of the tape by including points (your commercial) but keep it short or with the touch of a finger your prospect can jump past your message and escape "voice mail jail." Thank the caller for calling you and express your regrets that you are not there to take the call. As a sales professional, call your voice mail every few hours (*3 hours minimum*, usually) so that *you* can differentiate yourself in your responsiveness to your clients.

In summary, if you get a tape: be prepared, include a benefit, keep it short/crisp. Also follow up with a letter and call back.

Hold Button

As a matter of practice don't put clients on hold or keep them waiting for an extended period of time—a few seconds seems like an eternity when waiting on the telephone. It's rude and annoying, and most clients resent it. When it is necessary to put clients on hold, tell them what you are going to do, why, and approximately how long it will take. Ask them if they would prefer to be called back.

However, there are times you can use the hold button to your advantage. For example, during a tough negotiation, you may need to cool an irate client (or yourself!), to give yourself time to think when you are caught off guard, to confer with another decision maker, or just to slow things down. You can offer clients any number of reasons for putting them on hold, but stick to the truth. For example, if you need time to think, you can say, "Will you please hold for a moment? I'll be back with you right away."

If you need to confer with someone, say so: "I'll have to check with my trader. I'll . . . " or, "I'm sorry. I am not familiar with that promotion. Where did you hear about it? Let me check with my manager, Mr. X. I'll be . . . "

Using the hold button can be a defense tactic — the equivalent of silence in a face-to-face negotiation. It can also be a value added, demonstrating to your clients that you are making an effort to help them. Even if you can't comply, it helps you avoid saying no too quickly.

Be sure to get back to your client promptly. If you cannot regroup or replan in fewer than 30 seconds, ask the client if he or she wishes to hold or if you can have a manager call back. Whenever you return to a client who has been holding say, "Thank you for waiting. I . . . " Never, never leave the client connected while you are "off" the line. If you don't have a hold button, you may need to change your phone system!

Negotiating over the Telephone

When you find yourself having to negotiate or settle one point of a deal over the telephone, first and foremost make sure the telephone is the best medium. Factors to consider are covered in the Four Rs (Chap. 15), but keep in mind two key points in making the judgment: (1) how important is the negotiation and (2) how much attention do you want to place on the points being negotiated. In general, if the negotiation is very important, and if you really must avoid a no, don't use the telephone. It is easier for clients (or any one) to say no over the telephone than face-to-face. However, as mentioned, if you want to trivialize a point, the telephone may be the perfect tool. One West Coast senior manager called an East Coast colleague on a Friday afternoon. The two had an agreement already in place, but, along with talking about sailing, the weekend, the weather, one party was able to "slip" in a minor change that upon examination was *far* from minor. This executive used his "casual" call to get a concession at no cost to him. Remember too the investment banker who refused to let his team connect with a client because he did not want to magnify the client's demand — his strategy was to wait and deal with it at the last minute.

To help ensure that you don't leave money or terms on the table, use the following guidelines:

- Be prepared. Develop a list of your negotiation points; establish your essentials (what you must have) and your expendables (what you can trade). Remember it is easy to make *mistakes* over the telephone, so have your list ready and keep referring to it.

- Be the caller. If you are not prepared to negotiate, don't take the call unless you have to.

- Recognize that you are in a negotiation, and don't negotiate too soon if you are not ready. The moment your client begins to talk about price and terms, you are entering a negotiation. Ask yourself if you are ready to negotiate; being ready means (1) you know your client's needs, (2) the client knows the value you bring, (3) you have prepared for the negotiation — set an objective, bottom line, and so on.

- Don't assume because the telephone is the medium that the point the client is negotiating is trivial. As mentioned, the telephone can be used to win a concession by minimizing its importance.

- Be aware of the powers and pitfalls of team negotiation via conference calls. (See Telephone Conference Calls in this chapter.)

- Use the hold button if you need time. It is the technological equivalent of silence. But be careful in what you say: Don't assume that the hold button is working.

- Be *silent* after you state your price or terms. Silence is *very* powerful, *especially* over the telephone in a negotiation. The first to speak after price is stated is usually the first to fold!

- If you are calling for collection purposes call earlier rather than later, keep on-going contact, have a clear objective for each call in mind, end on an agreed action step, and keep things positive as long as you wish to maintain communication.

- Take lots of notes to use during the negotiation and for reference later on.

- Make sure *you* are the one to write up a summary of the call so you are in control of how things are positioned.

- Don't make agreements on the spot unless you are absolutely ready to make the commitment. Say, "Let me give that some thought. . . . "

- Don't use the telephone if you really cannot afford to get a no from the client, since it is much easier for a client to say no over the telephone than face-to-face.

- Check, ask questions. Don't assume that silence from the client means agreement.

- Convert demands to needs by asking why.

- Ask questions and listen. Use the objection resolution model (Chap. 4).

Keeping Your Support Staff
Informed/Involved

Your administrative support is key to how well you can respond to and service your clients. For example, if you think your prospect or client is about to make a decision about your proposal during the week, day, or hour you will be out of your office or away from your telephone, be sure to alert your office staff or secretary to how you can be reached. If you have a sales or office manager, communicate with him or her too. Whether you are away on business, on vacation, out to lunch, or simply away from your desk—for example, on another floor in your organization working on the deal—a support staff that isn't prepared to handle an inquiry or to locate you can cost you the deal.

One salesperson did *almost* everything right. He presented the right idea, he tailored his proposals, and he made follow-up telephone calls. As a result, he became one of two finalists for a big contract. But the day the client was making the decision, he was away on a well-deserved holiday. The client called with a last-minute pricing question. A temp took the message at 1:15 p.m. The salesperson found the message in his bin on Monday at 8:30 a.m.—too late. The competitor, who was there when the client needed him, had won the account. On another occasion, a banker was busy working out the details of a Eurobond deal with her colleagues in the credit department, as her client, the president of a *Fortune* 100 company, called and called and called, anxious to find out the status of the deal. Unfortunately, the secretary did not even know about the deal and could only say, "She is out." Luckily at 5:45 p.m. the banker returned to her desk and was able to assure the irate client that they were still interested in the deal and that documents were on their way to his office. The stress caused to the president and the jeopardy to the deal both could have been avoided. Secretaries can be invaluable if you take the time to communicate: Share your ideas, priorities, schedule, and thinking with them.

Without administrative support, you can lose deals that otherwise should have been won. In today's time-pressured, competitive environment, responsiveness is a *must*. It is impossible for you to be there personally every second. But you can set up a system in which your support people are there for you. For example, in investment banking firms there are "tape-watching" groups whose sole job is to yank key salespeople assigned to particular accounts out of meetings—off ski slopes, if necessary—if one of their clients goes into play so the salespeople can position themselves and not lose the opportunity.

To make sure clients can get answers to their questions, tell your sales manager and all secretaries in your group—yours in particular—the name of the client and the client's organization and which decision is pending. Indicate to your group when, where, and how you can be reached. Make sure temps who may be coming in are aware of this. Call clients to let them know you will not be in the office from X to Y (clients really appreciate this) and mention who to ask for in your absence. Of course, if appropriate, be sure to call the client on "D day" (decision day or week) yourself to see if the client has any final questions.

Including administrative assistants and secretaries in this process is an essential step—but one often overlooked. Many opportunities have slipped through the cracks because no one bothered to mention to these front-line players what deals were brewing. Secretaries who are briefed can be prepared to say, "Yes, John is away from his desk but I can reach him, Mr. Bryant." Or, if the salesperson is out of the office, "She is out of the office, but she will be calling in for messages . . . she will get back to you shortly. In the meantime, may I help you? May I take your questions? . . . What would be a good time . . . ?" or "I'm sorry she is not here. I know she was expecting your call. Can I have . . . ?" Of course if for some reason a secretary cannot reach a salesperson, the secretary should get to a manager (sales manager preferably) who could call the client immediately. One salesperson introduced his new sales associate to one of his clients, right before going on vacation. His rationale was to make sure this client was covered—"Let me introduce you to Sarah, my assistant. I'm going to let her connect into our call in a moment if that's okay with you so she knows the details and can assist you when I am not here. O.K.? Sarah, I'd like to introduce you to . . ."

Selling today requires teamwork involving seniors, specialists, associates, technicians, and administration. Don't forget a vital link—the secretary or administrative assistant—yours and the clients. Make sure your support staff is just that in how it handles the life line of your business, your phone. (See Chap. 20 for general office telephone etiquette.)

20
General Office Telephone Etiquette

The following are some general guidelines for your support/administrative team for telephone professionalism and etiquette:

Don't	Do
Don't let the telephone ring and ring and ring.	Always pick up the telephone by the *third* ring.
Don't answer the telephone by saying "Hello."	Say, "Good morning." "Good afternoon." Identify your company (if your company's protocol calls for it) and your name.
Don't wait to find out what the client wants. Don't just say, "May I help you?"	Ask, "*How* may I help you?" with a natural, friendly, but animated voice.
Don't be too casual or too informally friendly.	Be cordial and helpful. If the client says this is *John* Smith — unless otherwise directed — administrative staff should address the client by his or her surname (*Mr.* Smith). But administrative staff should refer to their own company's staff by their first or second names, not Mr. or Ms., unless

<u>Don't</u>	<u>Do</u>
	referring to the president or other high-ranking executive. "June Blake is not in the office, but she will be calling in. May I take a message?" Use Dr. or Rev. when appropriate.
Don't be canned.	*Listen* to what the client has to say and tailor your response accordingly.
Don't treat everything the same way.	Recognize an urgent situation. The client may say it is urgent or show that by calling back two or three times in a short time frame. After the second call back, take the message to a manager who can call the client back and try to help.
Don't put clients on hold or transfer calls without explaining what you are doing.	When you have to *transfer* a call, *tell the caller what you are going to do:* "Please hold, Mr. Smith, while I ring Ms. Wilson."
	Confirm that the person you plan to transfer the call to is available first.
	Announce to him or her who the client is on the other line and give your internal colleague the information you have about the caller.
	If you are trying to find the person, get back to the caller and keep him or her posted within 30 seconds.
	If the party is not there, take a message from the caller.
If after trying to find the right party you still cannot help the client, give the client the number to call for himself or herself.	Be responsible for getting the client to the right party. Make the connection, whenever possible, yourself. Ask the next party to call the client back.

Don't

Don't leave a client on hold for more than 30 seconds.

Don't keep the caller in the dark.

If your colleague or manager is not in the office, don't reveal to the caller where he or she is:

Don't say, "He or she is gone (has left) for the day." This says to the caller the person is not a "worker"— especially if you say this at noon or on a Friday in the summer!

Never say he or she is in the bathroom!

Do

If the client is on hold, get back to him or her within 20 or 30 seconds and give a status report: "Sorry to keep you on hold. Hank Wilson will be right with you."

One minute seems like an eternity. Get back on the line to the caller and let him or her know what is going on and find out if he or she cares to wait or be called back.

When you get back, say, "I apologize for keeping you waiting," or "Thank you for waiting."

If you must keep the client on hold for a few minutes, offer the client the option of your calling him or her back. Set the time and call back as promised.

Tell the client what you are going to do and get an okay to do it.

Do say, "John Smith is not here. He will be calling for messages on . . ." or "John Smith is away from his desk. He will be back soon. How may I help you or may I take a message?" If the client asks, "Where is he?" say, "I'm sorry, Mr. X, I do not have that information. May I take a message? Or can someone else help you?"

If asked where John Smith is, say, "I apologize. I do not have his schedule here. May I call you back?" Then check with management.

Don't	Do
Don't say, "She is in Chicago today." The smallest piece of information can be indiscrete and could give a competitor or client an important piece of information he or she should *not* have.	If it is a client John Smith knows very well, works with, and shares information with readily, you can check with him or her about what kind of information you can give.
Don't say he or she is on vacation or out on business *unless instructed to say so* — it is no one's business.	
Don't take a vague message.	Get the client's name, company, telephone number, *area code,* and message if the client wishes to leave one. Ask, "Would it save you some time if I could tell him or her what you are calling about when he or she calls in?" (Based on your company procedures or arrangements, you may ask if someone else may help the client, etc.)
Don't assume you got the information correctly or you got all the information.	Repeat the telephone number etc. to make sure you have the right information. Ask clients to spell their last names, if necessary. Make a point to learn names and affiliations of clients you *should* know so that you don't have to check spelling or ask for the caller's company. Even if you *think* you have the caller's telephone number, check. Say, "Mr. X, are you at your Philadelphia office?" You may be surprised that today he is in Pittsburgh. Don't make assumptions. Ask about area codes and times.
Don't say "Who are you with?"	Be more polite and say, "Mr. X, may I ask the name of your company?" More important, as mentioned, be-

Don't	Do
	come familiar with the names and affiliations of your clients, so that when you hear the caller's name you will know without asking what to write. Also, you can make the caller feel important: "Oh yes. Mr. Smith of Power Tools." If the caller does not give his or her name say, "May I ask who is calling?"
Don't sound like a prosecuting attorney.	Get the information in a positive, friendly, fast way.
Don't merely take a message if you can also help the client.	If the caller needs something you can handle, be proactive. For example, if a client did not receive a copy of a document such as a receipt, offer to send one and advise the salesperson. Of course, follow your company's policy regarding confidential information. Never send information that would compromise your organization or that is not absolutely directly related to the client.
Don't get defensive or hostile when called by an irate client.	Say "I apologize" (apologize for the situation) and then work to solve the problem by showing empathy, asking a question to get the information you need, positioning your response, and checking if your response satisfied the caller. Remain helpful. Be sure to tell the caller what your next step will be. If the situation seems urgent and the individual the caller is trying to reach is not in, get the call to the appropriate manager or salesperson. Be empathetic throughout but *do not make a commitment about what your company will or will not do.*

Don't	Do
Don't do what is convenient for you.	Be helpful even if it means getting up for a second and looking around for the person being called. Of course, don't leave telephones unattended for more than a few moments.
Don't let the caller control the call. If you are taking a message, don't just take what the client gives you. However, avoid offending the client or taking too much time.	Tactfully ask the caller for the information you need: ask who, what, when, where. Then summarize. Preface your questions to soften them. Tell the caller the reason for each question, showing a benefit whenever possible. For example, "So that I can look into this and have it ready for X, may I ask. . . . "
Again, you are not a D.A. or the CIA screening the client — you are trying to help the client.	
Don't use long or casual language. Don't use "yea," "OK," "sure," "thanks," etc.	Use standard English. Say, "yes," "certainly," "thank you."
Overall, don't be negative or impatient. Don't be a message taker.	Overall, maintain an attitude of helpfulness. Be courteous, competent, and show you care. Create a positive, professional image for your organization and yourself!

21
Final Tips for Telephone Selling

Some tips to help you sell on the telephone follow.

Preparing for the Telephone Sales Call

- Create your call list the night before so that you can maximize prime calling time.

- Plan a measurable objective or purpose for each telephone sales call.

- Do your homework. Be ready to sell.

- Clearly outline what you will say; eliminate mumbo jumbo.

- Make sure, based on your knowledge of the situation and client, that your idea applies to the client.

- Plan how you will tailor your idea to the client: Think of *three compelling reasons* that the client should do the deal or trade or buy from you.

- Be prepared for objections.

  What might the objections be? Play devil's advocate and get around your own no.

  "It's not for us."

"We don't want to. . . . "
"I already have. . . . "

- If you have three different pieces of information to present to a client, decide whether you want to present them all at once to make an "impact" or "power" call, or to use them to make three separate calls. With clients who are young MBA-types, the second tactic seems to work better, since it gives you multiple "real" reasons for contacting them.

- Plan client calls based on the client's preferences and needs: Find out *how* and when the client likes to be called, and note this in your tickler system.

- Keep your information—notes, files, competitor screen—in front of you. This is one of the *key* advantages of using the telephone.

- Clear your desk of other materials. Have your client files, telephone contact sheets, pens, calculators, rate sheets, product information, etc., on hand.

- *Dedicate blocks of time*—enough to get through your list.

Calling the Client

- Call top accounts first, working from your priority list. When calling with a new idea or new information, call a "give-and-take" client first so you can test newness before calling your top accounts who may not be as close to you. Better to hear, "Morgan called us *yesterday* (or, worse, *last* week) about that . . . " from a friend than from a critic.

- Qualify! Check to make sure you are reaching the right person—decision maker or influencer.

- Make a second and third effort.

- Use the six critical skills.

- Take notes of all important needs and details of the telephone conversation.

- Ask questions—find out *why*, especially when the client does not think the idea or product fits.

- Give information as well as get it.

- Ask for your action step.

- Keep energy in your voice. *Stand up* if it helps when you are on the telephone to increase your energy. Pace if necessary while you sell on the telephone. Stay focused. If you are slouched back in your chair all day, it is unlikely that you are selling!

- *Smile!* You can hear a smile in someone's voice. Words alone cannot make the sale; the tone of your voice makes a big difference. Imagine that the client is sitting in front of you and act accordingly. Be friendly, pleasant, upbeat, and focus on the client. This is one of the most important elements of effective telephone selling.

- Maximize your time. Some of the most effective telephone sales calls are relatively brief. Remember the top performer who uses a 1-minute egg timer so that he can get to all his key clients in a timely way.

- Be natural. Speak in a conversational manner and talk at a comfortable pace — not too fast, not too slow. No client likes to feel that he or she is being presented with a "canned" script. Talk on the same level as the client. Listen to the client's tone and pace and in a natural way emulate it, especially if you feel rapport is lacking. Establish rapport by using empathetic phrases such as "I can understand that" and "I know what you mean." Use the client's words, your client-tailored ideas, and the telephone format (opening . . . close) as a process.

- *Show good telephone manners.* Never smoke, eat, or drink while you are on the telephone. It is very annoying to hear someone inhaling smoke, chewing, or tinkling ice! Once you present a potential benefit, ask the client if this is a convenient time to call. Say thank you — whether or not you achieved your objective.

- Personalize the call. Use the client's name — more than once. Listen and incorporate clients' ideas and words, but don't overdo it!

- Boost the client's ego. Say, "Thank you for your time."

- Don't be impatient.

- Listen! Many people think they're at a disadvantage when using the telephone because they cannot pick up on body language. However, verbal cues can be very revealing. The tone and pattern of clients' speech can tell you a lot about them. *Listen* to what your client says and doesn't say. Read between the lines and you will gain insight into how to sell to each client.

- Be prepared. For example, have information next to you to indicate some depth ("It peaked in 1980").

- If your (your company's) opinion is different from the others, point it out by prefacing. For example, "I know the conservative estimate is X." Then say, "We think . . . "

- Give three reasons (at least) that a client should act on your idea; get client feedback as you present each reason. Use ideas one at a time.

- Keep a matrix for the day's phone calls: Why call was made, when placed, client reaction.

- *Follow up* properly on any client request for information.

- Be accurate. Telephones usually mean "quick," and quick means mistakes! Use your calculator and repeat agreements for confirmation. If you are not prepared to make a commitment, don't! Tell the client you'll get back to him or her.

- Be honest. No one has all the answers all the time. If you don't know the answer to a question, tell the client you'll check it out and set a time to get back to her or him.

- Create dialogue. Involve the client in the conversation. Question.

- Don't be discouraged if someone is rude. Don't take it personally. The worst thing that can happen is that someone will hang up on you. If this does happen, it says something about the client, not you. Use the objection resolution model to turn the situation around whenever possible.

- Keep prospecting. Many *experienced* salespeople take a small percentage of their time to make calls to prospects as a way to make sure the pipeline stays filled and to keep themselves on their toes. Prospecting is also valuable for new salespeople, since it helps them become comfortable on the telephone and sharpens their skills in getting through gatekeepers.

- While you are in a prospecting mode, experiment with new ideas as well as new people by taking about 10 percent of your prospects to try out new ideas and approaches. Again, this is a good exercise for new salespeople.

- Understand and respect the concept of a hit ratio. Remember, "You can't win 'em all." Telephone selling takes *perseverance!* Not all clients will take the desired action, but your goal is to get the maximum number of clients to say yes *to you.* Do not be discouraged if you have a string of "not interesteds." If you keep going and use your skills, they will begin to work in your favor.

- Remember the "learning curve": The more calls you make, the more practiced and comfortable you will be, and the greater your results.

- Call clients the day after a major presentation to thank them, and then ask if they have any questions.

- Call the client after your competitor has presented to see if your client has any questions (really to undo any misinformation or doubts created by the competitor.)

- Call your client on Friday afternoon about 2:30 in the summer. Most clients are apt to be at their desks, hoping to bail out early.

- Call your client before and/or after any important event such as a board meeting.

- Offer your clients your home telephone number when appropriate, especially in urgent situations. Clients who feel close to you may offer theirs in return. You can get insight into clients by their answering machine messages.

- If you really believe in service, instruct your secretary to give your home telephone number to clients in urgent situations who need to speak to you when you are out, especially if they leave their home numbers for you.

- Ask for referrals. Have prospects call your referrals. Also have referrals contact your prospects.
- Keep in mind what your clients want: performance, quality, and a trusting relationship.

Conclusion

Telephone selling is fraught with limitations. It can have an ominous quality about it. It can depersonalize. But in spite of these potential disadvantages, telephone selling can be an excellent way to build and strengthen relationships with clients. Whether you are making a relationship call simply to say hello, a business call to do a deal, or a combination of both, you can make the telephone work for you, not against you. You will find with skillful practice that telephone selling is an extraordinary sales tool.

The telephone can be the next best thing to being there, or it can be better—the method of choice in many situations. The difference lies mainly in your skill level and attitude toward telephone selling. Because physical cues are missing, you need to refine—make virtually perfect—your listening and your questioning skills. If your "radar" is down, you will miss the subtle signals that can lead you to success. If you associate telephone sales with the annoying telemarketing calls you get hawking products for which you truly have no need (or you do need, but you resent the caller so much it doesn't matter), then you will relegate the telephone to a lesser role. You will miss countless opportunities—to get to know your clients, give them unparalleled service, deliver on your sales promises, and increase your production. Whether you use the telephone to sell most of the day or to supplement your face-to-face contacts, you can differentiate yourself by literally "spoiling" your clients. Call. Call more often. Manage each moment to put the focus where it belongs—on helping your clients succeed—and you will share in their success.

Index

About the Author

Linda Richardson is the president of The Richardson Company, located in Philadelphia, Pennsylvania. The company provides custom-tailored sales training (sales, negotiations, sales management) to leading companies such as Morgan Stanley, NCNB, NBD, Citicorp, Swiss Bank, CoreStates, The Hartford, IBM, 3M, Johnson & Johnson, Winthrop Pharmaceuticals, and Tiffany & Co. Ms. Richardson pioneered the concept of customer-focused selling and win-win negotiations in the seventies and is an international leader in the field of sales and sales management excellence.

Ms. Richardson is the author of five books on selling and negotiating. She is also an adjunct professor at the Wharton Graduate School of the University of Pennsylvania and a frequent speaker at national sales and training conferences.